simple dinners

photography by William Meppem

Reproduction by News PreMedia Centre
Printed in China by RR Donnelley on 157gsm Matt Art
10 9 8 7 6 5 4 3 2 1

First published by HarperCollins*Publishers* Australia, Sydney, Australia, in 2011.
This United Kingdom edition published by arrangement with HarperCollins*Publishers*
Australia Pty Limited, in 2012.

Hardie Grant Books (UK)
Dudley House, North Suite, 34-35 Southampton Street,
London WC2E 7HF
www.hardiegrant.co.uk

Hardie Grant Books (Australia)
Ground Floor, Building 1, 658 Church Street,
Melbourne VIC 3121
www.hardiegrant.com.au

ISBN: 9781 7427 0434 0

on the cover
pasta wth chorizo, tomato and basil, page 40

donna hay

simple dinners

140+ new recipes, clever ideas and speedy solutions for every day

hardie grant books

MELBOURNE · LONDON

contents

*Ingredients marked with an asterisk have a glossary entry

introduction

How many times have you opened the pantry or fridge door and thought there's nothing to eat? This book is your saviour. Whether it's noodles or rice from the pantry or vegies from the fridge, I'll show you how to take everyday star ingredients and turn them into delicious weeknight dinners.

I've always been of the school that if you have an egg in the fridge, you have a meal on the table. I feel the same way about many pantry items and fresh staples, from bread and pasta to canned beans and couscous. If you have these versatile basics on hand, all you need to do is grab a few fresh vegies or herbs on your way home and you have a quick and flavoursome dinner on the table.

This book is proof that the simplest things are often the best. Like classic flavour combinations that deliver big results with minimal effort, old standbys given a makeover, or a shortcut to a family favourite. I hope it changes the way you think about cooking and makes weeknight dinners the simple and enjoyable affair they should be. Happy cooking.

Donna

eggs

caramelised onion and potato frittata

The egg yolk creates an instant silky sauce for the pasta and is a great partner for the pancetta.

soft egg and crispy pancetta pasta

caramelised onion and potato frittata

4 starchy potatoes, thickly sliced
1¼ cups (310ml) chicken stock
2 teaspoons rosemary leaves
½ cup (170g) store-bought caramelised onion relish*
6 eggs
1½ cups (375ml) single (pouring) cream*
sea salt and cracked black pepper
hot buttered toast, to serve

Place the potatoes, stock and rosemary in a non-stick frying pan over medium–high heat, cover, and cook for 12–14 minutes or until potatoes are tender. Uncover and cook for a further 4 minutes or until most of the stock has evaporated. Spoon the onion relish over the potato.

Whisk together the eggs, cream, salt and pepper and pour over the potato. Cook over low heat for 6–8 minutes or until the frittata is just starting to set. Place under a preheated hot grill (broiler) and cook for 5–7 minutes or until the frittata is set and golden. Cut into wedges and serve with hot buttered toast. SERVES 4.

soft egg and crispy pancetta pasta

400g spaghetti
1 tablespoon olive oil
4 cloves garlic, thinly sliced
1 x 125g piece flat pancetta*, finely chopped
1 cup sage leaves
finely grated parmesan and cracked black pepper, to serve
4 soft-boiled eggs

Cook the pasta in a large saucepan of salted boiling water over high heat for 8–10 minutes or until al dente.

While the pasta is cooking, heat the oil in a large non-stick frying pan over medium heat. Add the garlic, pancetta and sage and cook for 4–6 minutes or until the pancetta is golden. Drain the pasta, add to the pancetta mixture and toss to combine. Divide the pasta between plates and sprinkle generously with parmesan and pepper. Break a soft boiled egg over each plate to serve. SERVES 4.

thai shredded egg salad

150g green or yellow beans, trimmed and halved lengthways
3 cucumbers, sliced lengthways
1 cup mint leaves
1 cup basil leaves
1 cup coriander (cilantro) leaves
2 long red chillies*, seeds removed and thinly sliced
¼ cup (60ml) lime juice
¼ cup (60ml) fish sauce*
2 tablespoons caster (superfine) sugar
4 eggs
2 teaspoons sesame oil
roasted unsalted cashews, to serve

Place the beans in a heatproof bowl, cover with boiling water and stand for 3 minutes. Drain and refresh under cold water. Place the beans, cucumber, mint, basil, coriander and chilli in a large bowl. Combine the lime juice, fish sauce and sugar, pour over the salad and toss to combine. Divide the salad between plates.

Heat a quarter of the oil in large non-stick frying pan over high heat. Whisk one egg at a time and pour into the hot pan, swirling the pan to thinly coat the base. Cook for 1 minute or until set. Remove from the pan and repeat with remaining oil and eggs. Roll up each egg pancake, slice and serve with the salad and cashews. SERVES 4.

This is my version of pad Thai – without the noodles. It's light, crunchy and tangy with silky ribbons of egg tossed through.

thai shredded egg salad

soufflé omelette

3 eggs, separated
1 eggwhite, extra
2 tablespoons single (pouring) cream*
⅓ cup (65g) fresh ricotta
¼ cup (20g) finely grated parmesan
sea salt and cracked black pepper
butter, for frying
hot buttered toast, to serve

Place the egg yolks, cream, ricotta, parmesan, salt and pepper in a bowl and whisk until smooth. Place the 4 eggwhites in a separate bowl and whisk until stiff peaks form. Gently fold the eggwhites through the egg yolk mixture.

Heat a medium-sized non-stick frying pan over medium–low heat. Add a little butter and pour in half the egg mixture. Cook for 5 minutes or until the egg is set. Fold the omelette over and remove from the pan. Repeat with remaining mixture and serve omelettes with hot buttered toast. SERVES 2.

moroccan eggs

¾ cup (210g) thick plain yoghurt
1 clove garlic, crushed
2 large pieces Turkish (flat) bread*, halved
olive oil, for brushing
2 cups baby spinach leaves
store-bought green olive tapenade*, to serve
8 eggs, poached
2 teaspoons za'atar*

Place the yoghurt and garlic in a bowl and mix to combine. Set aside. Brush the Turkish bread with a little olive oil and char-grill until golden. Top the toast with the spinach leaves, a little green olive tapenade and the poached eggs and sprinkle with the za'atar. Serve with the garlic yoghurt. SERVES 4.

ricotta egg fritters

4 eggs, separated
½ cup (75g) self-raising (self-rising) flour, sifted
½ cup (125ml) milk
1¾ cups (350g) fresh ricotta
1 cup (80g) finely grated parmesan
2 tablespoons chopped chives
sea salt and cracked black pepper
butter, for frying
12 slices round pancetta*, grilled

Place the egg yolks, flour and milk in a bowl and mix until smooth.
Add the ricotta, parmesan, chives, salt and pepper and stir to
combine. Place the eggwhites in a separate bowl and beat until stiff
peaks form. Gently fold the eggwhite through the ricotta mixture.

 Melt a little butter in a large non-stick frying pan over medium-low
heat. Add ¼ cupfuls of the mixture to the pan and cook, in batches,
for 2–3 minutes each side or until the fritters are puffed and golden.
Divide fritters between plates and top with the pancetta. Serve with
a rocket (arugula), basil and parmesan salad, if desired. SERVES 4.

baked pancetta brioche with thyme mushrooms

4 brioche* buns
8 slices round pancetta*
3 eggs
½ cup (125ml) single (pouring) cream*
½ cup (60g) grated gruyère* cheese
sea salt and cracked black pepper
8 field mushrooms
melted butter, for brushing
2 tablespoons thyme leaves

Preheat oven to 200°C (400°F). Cut rounds out of the tops of the
brioche buns and remove some of the soft brioche inside to create
a hole and discard. Line the insides of the buns with the pancetta.
Place the eggs, cream and cheese in a bowl, sprinkle with salt and
pepper and whisk to combine. Pour the egg mixture into the brioche
buns and place on a baking tray lined with non-stick baking paper.
Add the mushrooms to the tray, brush with butter and sprinkle with
thyme and extra salt. Bake for 20–25 minutes or until golden and the
egg has set. Serve the brioche buns with the mushrooms. SERVES 4.

smashed pea, goat's cheese and egg bruschetta

smoked ham and potato hash with poached eggs

smashed pea, goat's cheese and egg bruschetta

2½ cups (300g) frozen peas
¼ cup chopped mint leaves
1 teaspoon finely grated lemon rind
1 tablespoon lemon juice
1 tablespoon olive oil
sea salt and cracked black pepper
8 slices crusty bread
olive oil, extra, for brushing and drizzling
250g soft goat's cheese*
8 eggs, poached
mint leaves, extra, to serve

Place the peas in a heatproof bowl and cover with boiling water. Allow to stand for 1 minute, drain and refresh under cold water. Return the peas to the bowl and roughly mash with a fork. Add the mint, lemon rind and juice, oil, salt and pepper. Brush the bread with the extra oil and char-grill until golden. Spread the bread with the goat's cheese and spoon the pea mixture over the cheese. Top with the poached eggs and extra mint, sprinkle with salt and pepper and drizzle with a little oil, to serve. SERVES 4.

smoked ham and potato hash with poached eggs

1.5kg starchy potatoes, peeled and grated
150g butter, melted
¾ cup flat-leaf parsley leaves
150g double smoked ham, shredded
sea salt and cracked black pepper
100g watercress sprigs
8 eggs, poached
horseradish cream
½ cup (120g) sour cream
2 tablespoons store-bought grated horseradish*

Place the potatoes, butter, parsley, ham, salt and pepper in a bowl and mix to combine. Heat a large non-stick frying pan over medium-low heat. Place large spoonfuls of the mixture into the pan, flatten, and cook for 6 minutes each side or until golden and crisp.

To make the horseradish cream, combine the sour cream and horseradish. Layer the potato hash and watercress on plates and top with the poached egg. Serve with horseradish cream. SERVES 4.

bacon egg rolls

8 rashers smoked bacon, rind removed
400g truss cherry tomatoes
8 eggs
⅓ cup (80ml) single (pouring) cream*
sea salt and cracked black pepper
store-bought tomato relish and hot buttered toast, to serve

Preheat oven to 200°C (400°F). Place the bacon and tomatoes on a tray lined with non-stick baking paper and roast for 15 minutes or until the bacon is crisp.

Place 2 eggs, 1 tablespoon of the cream, salt and pepper in a bowl and whisk to combine. Heat a large non-stick frying pan over high heat. Pour the egg mixture into the pan and swirl to coat the pan. Cook for 45–60 seconds or until the egg is just cooked. Turn onto a plate and top with tomato relish and 2 rashers of bacon. Roll to enclose and repeat with remaining eggs, relish and bacon. Sprinkle with pepper and serve with hot buttered toast and the oven-roasted tomatoes. SERVES 4.

spicy chickpea and chorizo fried eggs

4 chorizo*, sliced
2 red onions, sliced into thin wedges
2 tablespoons brown sugar
1 tablespoon red wine vinegar
3 tablespoons oregano leaves
1 x 400g can chickpeas (garbanzos), drained
4 eggs
1 teaspoon smoked paprika*
1 teaspoon sea salt flakes
shredded lemon zest, flat-leaf parsley leaves and
    hot buttered toast, to serve

Heat a large non-stick frying pan over high heat. Add the chorizo and cook for 5–7 minutes or until golden, remove from the pan and set aside. Add the onions to the pan and cook, stirring, for 8 minutes or until golden. Add the sugar and vinegar and cook for a further 2 minutes. Return the chorizo to the pan with the oregano and chickpeas and cook for a further 4 minutes. Make 4 holes in the chorizo mixture and break an egg into each hole. Reduce heat to medium–low and cook, covered, for 4 minutes or until the eggs are cooked to your liking. Combine the paprika and salt and sprinkle over the eggs. Serve with lemon zest, parsley and toast. SERVES 4.

Here is my chic version of the classic bacon and egg roll for a lazy weeknight dinner.

bacon egg rolls

This gutsy Spanish-style dish
does double duty as a quick
dinner or a generous breakfast.

spicy chickpea and chorizo fried eggs

tips & tricks

RIGHT
The perfect soft-boiled egg should be boiled for exactly 6 minutes for a luscious runny yolk. Make sure you start with cold water.

BELOW
To make sure the yolks are perfectly centred in boiled eggs, stir the water when you are bringing the eggs to the boil.

I'm of the school that if you have an egg in the fridge, you have a meal on the table. They're great for easy frittatas, omelettes, salads and more.

ABOVE
To tell if an egg is fresh, place it in a glass of water. If it sinks to the bottom on its side, it's fresh. The older the egg, the more it will float.

LEFT
For a nicely poached egg without the flyaway strands, add a tablespoon of vinegar to the poaching water to help the egg hold its shape.

bread

Celeriac is the new slaw. It's all about the creamy crunch with the golden crumbed chicken.

simple chicken schnitzel sandwich

roasted pumpkin, blue cheese and pear bruschetta

simple chicken schnitzel sandwich

1½ cups (105g) fresh breadcrumbs
60g butter, melted
½ cup (40g) finely grated parmesan
sea salt and cracked black pepper
2 x 200g chicken breast fillets, trimmed and halved lengthways
4 bread rolls, halved
slaw
700g celeriac (celery root), peeled and thinly sliced
½ cup flat-leaf parsley leaves
⅓ cup (100g) whole-egg mayonnaise
2 tablespoons lemon juice

Place the breadcrumbs, butter, parmesan, salt and pepper in a bowl and mix to combine. Place the chicken on a greased baking tray and top with the breadcrumb mixture. Cook the chicken under a preheated hot grill (broiler) for 4–5 minutes or until the chicken is cooked through and the crumbs are golden.

To make the slaw, place the celeriac and parsley in a bowl. Add the mayonnaise and lemon juice and toss to combine. Top the bread rolls with the slaw and chicken to serve. SERVES 4.

roasted pumpkin, blue cheese and pear bruschetta

1.5kg butternut pumpkin (squash), peeled and chopped
2 tablespoons olive oil
1 cup sage leaves
4 large (or 8 small) slices sourdough bread
olive oil, extra, for brushing
¾ cup (210g) store-bought caramelised onion relish*
150g blue cheese*
60g wild rocket (arugula) leaves
1 firm brown pear, thinly sliced with a mandolin
⅓ cup (35g) walnuts, toasted

Preheat oven to 200°C (400°F). Place the pumpkin, oil and sage in a baking dish and toss to combine. Bake for 30 minutes or until the pumpkin is soft and golden.

Brush the bread with a little oil and char-grill or toast until crisp. Place on a baking tray lined with non-stick baking paper and spread with the onion relish. Top the bread with the pumpkin, sage and blue cheese, place under a preheated hot grill (broiler) and grill for 2 minutes or until the cheese has melted. Top with the rocket, pear and walnuts to serve. SERVES 4.

harissa pumpkin and goat's cheese pizza

600g butternut pumpkin (squash), peeled and chopped
1 tablespoon harissa*
1 tablespoon olive oil
4 large flat breads*
2½ cups (500g) fresh ricotta
1¼ cups (350g) store-bought caramelised onion relish*
300g firm goat's cheese, crumbled
100g rocket (arugula) leaves
8 slices prosciutto

Preheat oven to 180°C (350°F). Place the pumpkin, harissa and oil in a bowl and toss to combine. Place the pumpkin on a baking tray lined with non-stick baking paper and roast for 15 minutes or until just starting to soften. Spread the flat bread with the ricotta and onion relish. Top with the pumpkin and goat's cheese and bake for a further 25 minutes or until golden. Top with rocket leaves and prosciutto to serve. SERVES 4.

Using thin flat bread as a pizza base gets a great crisp result but without the work. Plus, it's faster than dialling for takeaway.

harissa pumpkin and goat's cheese pizza

bread and butter bacon pudding

8 slices sourdough bread
80g butter
7 thin rashers bacon, rind removed and trimmed of excess fat
8 eggs
1¼ cups (310ml) milk
1¼ cups (155g) grated gruyère* cheese
1 tablespoon Dijon mustard
sea salt and cracked black pepper

Preheat oven to 180°C (350°F). Spread one side of the bread slices with the butter. Layer the bread in a 1.5 litre-capacity baking dish, placing the rashers of bacon between the bread slices. Place the eggs, milk, cheese, mustard, salt and pepper in a bowl and whisk to combine. Pour over the bread and bake for 30 minutes or until the bread is golden and the filling is just set. Serve with a simple green salad with a lemon dressing, if desired. SERVES 4.

sourdough chicken pies

2 cups (320g) chopped cooked chicken
¼ cup (60g) sour cream
¾ cup (180g) fresh ricotta
¼ cup chopped flat-leaf parsley leaves
1 teaspoon finely grated lemon rind
sea salt and cracked black pepper
16 slices soft white bread
80g butter, melted
sesame seeds, for sprinkling

Preheat oven to 200°C (400°F). Place the chicken, sour cream, ricotta, parsley, lemon rind, salt and pepper in a large bowl and mix to combine. Brush one side of each slice of bread with a little butter. Place half the slices, butter-side up, on a baking tray lined with non-stick baking paper. Divide the chicken filling between the bread and top with remaining bread slices, butter-side down. Press the edges of the bread together to seal and using a large cookie cutter, cut a round from the bread. Discard the crusts. Brush with a little more butter, sprinkle with sesame seeds and bake for 20 minutes or until golden and crunchy. Serve with a simple green salad, if desired. SERVES 4.

prosciutto, sage and ricotta french toast

1½ cups (300g) fresh ricotta
⅓ cup shredded basil leaves
1 cup (80g) finely grated parmesan
8 thick slices white bread
8 slices prosciutto
6 eggs, lightly beaten
¼ cup (60ml) milk
½ cup (40g) finely grated parmesan, extra
butter, for cooking
24 large sage leaves

Place the ricotta, basil and parmesan in a bowl and mix to combine. Spread the ricotta mixture over half the bread slices. Top with prosciutto and sandwich with remaining bread slices.

Place the eggs, milk and extra parmesan in a shallow dish and whisk to combine. Dip the sandwiches, one at a time, in the egg mixture for 30 seconds each side. Melt a little butter in a large non-stick frying pan over medium heat. Press 3 sage leaves into each side of a sandwich, place in the pan and cook for 2–3 minutes each side or until golden. Repeat with remaining sandwiches. Serve with a simple green salad, if desired. SERVES 4.

crunchy top beef pies

1 tablespoon olive oil
2 brown onions, sliced
1.2kg beef chuck steak, cut into 2cm cubes
2 tablespoons plain (all-purpose) flour
sea salt and cracked black pepper
2 cups (500ml) beef stock
1 cup (280g) tomato purée* (passata)
1 tablespoon Worcestershire sauce
250g crusty bread, roughly chopped
60g butter, melted
1 tablespoon rosemary leaves

Heat the oil in a large, deep non-stick frying pan over medium–high heat. Add the onions and cook for 6–8 minutes or until well browned. Set aside. Toss the beef in the flour, salt and pepper. Add to the pan and cook, in batches, for 6 minutes or until browned. Return all the meat to the pan along with the stock, tomato purée, Worcestershire and onions and bring to a simmer. Cover and cook for 1 hour or until the meat is tender. Preheat oven to 200°C (400°F). Spoon the beef mixture into 4 x 1½-cup (125ml) capacity pie dishes and top with the combined bread, butter and rosemary. Bake for 20 minutes or until golden. Serve with a mixed green salad, if desired. SERVES 4.

It's the perfect combination of crisp fennel and crunchy toasts with a lovely creamy dressing.

chicken and fennel salad with parmesan wafers

lemon, caper and tuna grilled sandwiches

chicken and fennel salad with parmesan wafers

2 bulbs fennel, thinly sliced
4 x 200g cooked chicken breast fillets, sliced
1 cup flat-leaf parsley leaves
1 cup mint leaves
½ cup (150g) whole-egg mayonnaise
¼ cup (60ml) lemon juice
sea salt and cracked black pepper
parmesan wafers
16 very thin slices baguette
75g butter, melted
1½ cups (120g) finely grated parmesan
2 tablespoons thyme leaves

Preheat oven to 180°C (350°F). To make the wafers, brush one side of the bread slices with butter and place on a baking tray lined with non-stick baking paper. Combine the parmesan and thyme and sprinkle over the bread. Bake for 8–10 minutes or until golden.

Place the fennel, chicken, parsley and mint in a bowl and toss to combine. Whisk together the mayonnaise, lemon juice, salt and pepper. Divide the salad between plates and pour over the dressing. Serve with parmesan wafers. SERVES 4.

lemon, caper and tuna grilled sandwiches

1 x 425g can tuna, drained
¾ cup (225g) whole-egg mayonnaise
1 tablespoon salted capers, rinsed and drained
1 teaspoon finely grated lemon rind
1 tablespoon chopped dill leaves
2 tablespoons chopped flat-leaf parsley leaves
sea salt and cracked black pepper
8 large slices wholemeal or light rye bread
olive oil, for brushing

Place the tuna, mayonnaise, capers, lemon rind, dill, parsley, salt and pepper in a bowl and mix to combine. Spread half the bread slices with the tuna mixture and sandwich with remaining bread slices. Brush both sides of the sandwiches with oil. Heat a char-grill pan or a sandwich press over medium heat. Placing a plate and a can of vegetables over the sandwich to flatten, cook the sandwich for 3 minutes each side or until crisp and golden. Repeat with remaining sandwiches. Serve with a radish and watercress salad, if desired. SERVES 4.

roasted tomato, garlic and bread salad

500g baby Roma tomatoes, halved
250g sourdough bread, roughly chopped
12 cloves garlic, skin on
2 tablespoons olive oil
2 tablespoons white balsamic vinegar
¼ cup (60ml) olive oil, extra
1 tablespoon white balsamic vinegar, extra
2 tablespoons water
4 cups (125g) baby rocket (arugula) leaves
12 slices prosciutto

Preheat oven to 160°C (325°F). Place the tomatoes, bread, garlic, oil and vinegar in a bowl and toss to combine. Place on a baking tray lined with non-stick baking paper and roast for 40 minutes or until the bread is crisp and golden. Remove the garlic from the tray and squeeze from its skin into a bowl. Add the extra oil, vinegar and water and mix to combine. Place the tomato and bread mixture in a bowl and toss with the rocket. Divide between plates, spoon over the roasted garlic dressing and top with prosciutto to serve. SERVES 4.

baked spicy beef quesadillas

16 store-bought flour tortillas
olive oil, for brushing
hot chilli sauce, sour cream, sliced avocado, lime wedges
    and coriander (cilantro) leaves, to serve
spicy beef filling
500g beef mince (ground beef)
1 x 400g can white (cannellini) beans, drained, rinsed and mashed
3 tablespoons tomato paste
½ cup chopped coriander (cilantro) leaves
¼ cup (60ml) hot chilli sauce
1½ cups (180g) finely grated aged cheddar

Preheat oven to 200°C (400°F). To make the spicy beef filling, place the mince, beans, tomato paste, coriander, chilli and cheddar in a large bowl and mix well to combine. Spread the beef mixture over half the tortillas and sandwich with remaining tortillas to enclose the filling. Brush both sides with oil and place on a baking tray lined with non-stick baking paper. Top with another baking tray and bake for 15 minutes or until the quesadillas are crisp and the filling is cooked through. Halve the quesadillas and serve with extra chilli sauce, sour cream, avocado, lime and coriander. SERVES 4.

Salad doesn't need to be subtle. Make it robust with peppery rocket and salty-sweet prosciutto.

roasted tomato, garlic and bread salad

baked spicy beef quesadillas

tips & tricks

RIGHT
When freezing a loaf of bread, pre-slice it and pop sheets of baking paper between every second slice for easy use.

BELOW
Keep a variety of different breads on hand in the freezer for quick pizzas, wraps, dinner bruschettas and more.

I love the versatility of bread and its uses beyond the classic sandwich in everything from soups and salads to pies and pizzas.

ABOVE
Don't drag out the food processor every time you need to make breadcrumbs. Make a big batch and freeze for easy convenience.

LEFT
As a quick guide, 2 slices of bread make 1 cup of breadcrumbs. If you're using a hard bread, make sure you remove the crust first.

pasta

cheat's ricotta gnocchi with sage butter

This pasta dish combines all the great flavours – salty, spicy, fresh and creamy in one satisfying bowl.

pasta wth chorizo, tomato and basil

cheat's ricotta gnocchi with sage butter

2½ cups (500g) fresh ricotta
½ cup (40g) finely grated parmesan
2 eggs, lightly beaten
1 cup (150g) plain (all-purpose) flour, sifted
½ teaspoon sea salt flakes
12 slices round pancetta*
40g butter
32 sage leaves
finely grated parmesan, extra, and cracked black pepper, to serve

Place the ricotta, parmesan, eggs, flour and salt in a bowl and mix well to combine. Divide the dough into 4 and roll each piece on a lightly floured surface into 30cm x 2cm long ropes. Cut into 3cm pieces and set aside.

To make the sauce, heat a non-stick frying pan over high heat. Add the pancetta and cook for 2 minutes each side or until golden and crisp. Remove from the pan and set aside. Add the butter and sage leaves and cook for 1 minute or until the sage is crisp.

Cook the gnocchi in a large saucepan of boiling salted water in small batches for 2–3 minutes or until the gnocchi float to the surface. Drain and keep warm. Divide the gnocchi between serving plates and top with the pancetta and sage butter. Top with extra parmesan and cracked black pepper to serve. SERVES 4.

pasta with chorizo, tomato and basil

vegetable oil, for frying
1 cup basil leaves
3 chorizo*, thinly sliced
500g truss cherry tomatoes
400g pappardelle
2 tablespoons olive oil
1 tablespoon finely grated lemon rind
1 clove garlic, crushed
sea salt and cracked black pepper
2 x 125g buffalo mozzarella*, torn
finely grated parmesan, to serve

Preheat oven to 200°C (400°F). Heat the oil in a small saucepan over high heat. Carefully add the basil leaves a few at a time, as they may spit, and fry until crisp. Drain on absorbent paper and set aside.

Place the chorizo and tomato on a baking tray lined with non-stick baking paper and roast for 15 minutes or until chorizo is golden. While the chorizo is roasting, cook the pasta in a saucepan of salted boiling water for 10–12 minutes or until al dente. Drain and keep warm.

Add the olive oil, lemon rind and garlic to the pan and cook for 1 minute. Return the pasta to the pan with the chorizo, tomato, salt and pepper and toss to combine. Divide the pasta between plates and top with the mozzarella, parmesan and fried basil leaves to serve. SERVES 4.

prawn spaghetti with lemon vodka sauce

400g spaghetti
20g butter
4 cloves garlic, sliced
20 green (raw) prawns (shrimp), peeled with tails intact
1 cup (250ml) single (pouring) cream
2 tablespoons vodka
2 tablespoons lemon juice
½ cup flat-leaf parsley leaves
sea salt and cracked black pepper

Cook the pasta in a large saucepan of salted boiling water for 10–12 minutes or until al dente. Drain and keep warm.

While the pasta is cooking, melt the butter in a non-stick frying pan over medium–high heat. Add the garlic and prawns and cook for 2 minutes, remove from the pan and set aside. Add the cream, vodka and lemon juice to the pan and simmer for 5 minutes. Return the prawns to the pan with the pasta, parsley, salt and pepper and toss to combine. SERVES 4.

The combination of lemon and vodka gives this sauce a subtle edge that's perfect with prawns.

prawn spaghetti with lemon vodka sauce

cheat's ravioli lasagne

1kg large good-quality cheese-filled ravioli
1 tablespoon olive oil
1 brown onion, chopped
2 cloves garlic, crushed
2 x 400g cans chopped tomatoes
1 cup (250ml) tomato purée* (passata)
½ cup torn basil leaves
sea salt and cracked black pepper
8 slices prosciutto
400g fresh ricotta
¼ cup (20g) finely grated parmesan

Preheat oven to 180°C (350°F). Cook the ravioli according to packet instructions, drain and set aside. Heat the oil in a non-stick frying pan over medium heat. Add the onion and garlic and cook for 3 minutes or until the onions are soft. Add the tomatoes and purée and simmer for 10 minutes or until the sauce has reduced. Stir through the basil, salt and pepper. To assemble, place half the ravioli in a greased 3-litre capacity ovenproof dish and top with half the tomato sauce and half the prosciutto slices. Repeat with remaining ravioli, tomato sauce and prosciutto. Top with ricotta and sprinkle with parmesan. Bake for 30 minutes or until golden. SERVES 4.

chicken and porcini pappardelle

30g dried porcini mushrooms*
1 cup (250ml) boiling water
400g pappardelle
1 tablespoon olive oil
1 clove garlic, crushed
½ cup small sage leaves
2 x 200g cooked chicken breast fillets, shredded
1 cup (250ml) single (pouring) cream*
sea salt and cracked black pepper
finely grated parmesan, to serve

Place the porcini in a bowl and cover with boiling water. Allow to stand for 5 minutes. Drain the porcini, reserving ¼ cup (60ml) soaking water, slice and set aside.

Cook the pasta in a large saucepan of boiling salted water for 10–12 minutes or until al dente. While the pasta is cooking, heat the oil in a non-stick frying pan over medium heat, add the garlic and sage and cook for 1 minute. Add the chicken and cream and cook for 2 minutes or until heated through. Add the sliced porcini, reserved soaking liquid, drained pasta, salt and pepper and toss to combine. Divide between plates and top with grated parmesan to serve. SERVES 4.

asparagus, pea and pecorino spaghetti

400g thin spaghetti
2 tablespoons olive oil
1 tablespoon finely grated lemon rind
1 long red chilli*, finely chopped
⅓ cup (80ml) vegetable or chicken stock
8 stalks asparagus, shaved with a vegetable peeler
1½ cups (180g) frozen peas, thawed
½ cup shredded mint leaves
1 cup finely shredded rocket (arugula) leaves
1 cup (80g) finely grated pecorino*
sea salt and cracked black pepper

Cook the pasta in a large saucepan of salted boiling water for
3–4 minutes or until al dente. Drain the pasta and keep warm.
Add the oil, lemon rind and chilli to the pan and cook for 1 minute.
Add the pasta, stock, asparagus, peas, mint and rocket and toss
to combine. Stir through the pecorino, salt and pepper and divide
between bowls to serve. SERVES 4.

summer caprese lasagne

12 x 10cm square fresh lasagne sheets
4 large vine-ripened tomatoes, sliced
1 cup basil leaves
2 x 125g large buffalo mozzarella*, sliced
2 cups (50g) rocket (arugula) leaves
¼ cup (60ml) olive oil
2 tablespoons red wine vinegar
sea salt and cracked black pepper
finely grated parmesan, to serve

Cook the pasta in a large saucepan of boiling salted water for
3–4 minutes or until al dente. Drain and rinse under warm water
to remove any surface starch and cool slightly.
    Place one sheet of cooked pasta on each plate and top with a
few slices of tomato and basil leaves. Top with another sheet of
pasta, a couple of slices of mozzarella and some rocket. Top with
a final sheet of pasta and the remaining tomato and basil. Combine
the oil, vinegar, salt and pepper and spoon over the lasagne. Serve
with parmesan. SERVES 4.

Tossed with garlic, pepper
and ricotta, this pasta is about
simplicity with plenty of flavour.

pepper and garlic fettucine with ricotta

beetroot and goat's cheese orecchiette

pepper and garlic fettucine with ricotta

400g fettucine
40g butter
4 cloves garlic, sliced
1½ teaspoons cracked black pepper
1 cup torn basil leaves
1¼ cups (250g) fresh ricotta
finely grated parmesan, to serve

Cook the pasta in a large saucepan of salted boiling water for
10–12 minutes or until al dente. Drain the pasta and keep warm.
Add the butter, garlic and pepper to the pan and cook for 2 minutes
or until fragrant. Return the pasta to the pan and toss to coat.
Stir through the basil and divide pasta between plates. Top with the
ricotta and sprinkle generously with parmesan to serve. SERVES 4.

beetroot and goat's cheese orecchiette

16 baby beetroot, trimmed, scrubbed and halved
¼ cup marjoram leaves
2 tablespoons olive oil
sea salt and cracked black pepper
400g orecchiette
1 tablespoon olive oil, extra
1 clove garlic, crushed
2 cups (50g) small beetroot leaves
1 cup (100g) grated firm goat's cheese*
olive oil, for drizzling

Preheat oven on 200°C (400°F). Toss together the beetroot,
marjoram, oil, salt and pepper and place on a baking tray lined with
non-stick baking paper. Bake for 30 minutes or until tender.
    While the beetroot is roasting, cook the pasta in a saucepan
of salted boiling water for 10–12 minutes or until al dente. Drain,
return to the warm pan and stir through the extra oil, garlic and
beetroot leaves. Cook over low heat for 1 minute or until warmed
through. Divide the pasta between bowls and top with the roasted
beetroot mixture, goat's cheese and a drizzle of olive oil to serve.
SERVES 4.

blt pasta

6 thin rashers bacon, rind removed
250g truss cherry tomatoes
400g spaghetti
1 cup (250ml) single (pouring) cream*
1 tablespoon finely grated lemon rind
1 cup basil leaves
2 cups (50g) baby rocket (arugula) leaves
finely grated parmesan, to serve

Preheat oven to 200°C (400°F). Place the bacon and tomatoes
on a baking tray lined with non-stick baking paper and roast for
15 minutes or until bacon is crisp. Break the bacon into large pieces.
    Cook the pasta in a large saucepan of salted boiling water for
10–12 minutes or until al dente. Drain the pasta and return to the
pan with the cream and lemon and toss to coat. Divide between
bowls and top with the bacon, tomatoes, basil and rocket. Sprinkle
with parmesan to serve. SERVES 4.

I've turned the classic BLT into a pasta with peppery rocket, crisp bacon and oven-roasted tomatoes.

spaghetti with chunky rocket pesto

400g spaghetti
finely grated parmesan and lemon wedges, to serve
chunky rocket pesto
4 cups (120g) shredded rocket (arugula) leaves
1 clove garlic, crushed
⅓ cup (80ml) olive oil
¼ cup (40g) pine nuts, toasted
⅓ cup (30g) finely grated parmesan
1 tablespoon finely grated lemon rind
sea salt and cracked black pepper

Cook the pasta in a large saucepan of boiling salted water for
10–12 minutes or until al dente. Drain and keep warm.
    While the pasta is cooking, make the pesto. Combine the rocket,
garlic, oil, pine nuts, parmesan, lemon rind, salt and pepper. Toss
through the warm pasta and top with extra grated parmesan and
a squeeze of lemon to serve. SERVES 4.

blt pasta

spaghetti with chunky rocket pesto

tips & tricks

RIGHT
You can use fresh or dried pasta in these recipes; fresh pasta cooks faster than dried and can have a silkier texture.

BELOW
Choose the right pasta shape for the right sauce. Short pasta is good for chunky sauces while long pasta is best for thinner sauces.

Pasta is the busy cook's best friend. It's quick and easy to prepare and lends itself as a base to infinite flavour combinations.

ABOVE
It's a kitchen myth that you should add oil to the cooking water. Oil and water don't mix and it won't prevent the pasta from sticking together.

LEFT
As a general guide, allow 100g dried pasta per person when serving a pasta dish.

noodles & rice

ginger fried rice with egg

This dish is about textures and flavours, from slippery noodles to spicy broth and sticky chicken.

chilli chicken noodles with spicy broth

ginger fried rice with egg

2 teaspoons sesame oil
1 tablespoon vegetable oil
1½ tablespoons finely grated ginger
4 cloves garlic, sliced
5 cups cooked jasmine rice (325g uncooked rice)
¼ cup (60ml) light soy sauce
4 eggs, fried
6 green onions (scallions), trimmed and sliced
2 long green or red chillies*, thinly sliced
½ cup coriander (cilantro) leaves
steamed bok choy* and hot chilli sauce, to serve

Heat both the oils in a large non-stick frying pan or wok over high heat. Add the ginger and garlic and cook for 2–3 minutes. Add the rice and cook, stirring, for 4–5 minutes or until heated through. Stir through the soy sauce. Divide the rice between plates and top with a fried egg, green onion, chilli and coriander. Serve with the bok choy and chilli sauce. SERVES 4.

chilli chicken noodles with spicy broth

200g dried rice noodles*
2 cups (500ml) chicken stock
2 tablespoons shredded ginger
2 long red chillies*, seeds removed and shredded
2 tablespoons Chinese cooking wine* (Shaoxing)
2 tablespoons chilli jam*
3 x 200g chicken breast fillets, trimmed and thinly sliced
coriander (cilantro) leaves and shredded green onion (scallion),
    to serve

Cook the noodles according to packet instructions and set aside. Place the stock, ginger, chilli and cooking wine in a saucepan over medium heat and bring to a simmer.
    Place the chilli jam and chicken in a bowl and toss to combine. Heat a non-stick frying pan over high heat. Add the chicken and cook, stirring, for 2–3 minutes or until cooked through. Divide the noodles between bowls and pour over the broth. Top with the chicken, coriander and green onion to serve. SERVES 4.

pea and mint risotto with crispy pancetta

1½ cups (180g) frozen peas
2 cups (400g) arborio (risotto) rice
1.25 litres (5 cups) chicken stock
1 tablespoon finely grated lemon rind
40g butter
½ cup (40g) finely grated parmesan
½ cup shredded mint leaves
sea salt and cracked black pepper
125g goat's curd or soft goat's cheese*
12 slices round pancetta*, grilled until crisp
finely grated parmesan, extra, to serve

Preheat oven to 200°C (400°F). Place the peas in a bowl, cover with boiling water and stand for 5 minutes. Drain and set aside.
    Place the rice, stock and lemon rind in a 3-litre capacity ceramic ovenproof dish. Cover tightly with aluminium foil and bake for 35 minutes. Remove from the oven and stir through the drained peas, butter, parmesan, mint, salt and pepper. Continue stirring for 5 minutes or until the risotto thickens and is creamy. Divide between plates and top with the goat's cheese, crispy pancetta slices and extra parmesan to serve. SERVES 4.

It's no secret I love a one-pan dish. This baked risotto is so easy to prepare and virtually cooks itself in the oven.

pea and mint risotto with crispy pancetta

crisp rice and crab omelette

2 tablespoons vegetable oil
2 cups cooked jasmine rice (130g uncooked rice)
2 teaspoons finely grated ginger
1 long red chilli*, chopped
6 green onions (scallions), trimmed and sliced
200g picked crab meat+
6 eggs, lightly beaten
1 cup coriander (cilantro) leaves
100g snow peas (mange tout), blanched and sliced
2 teaspoons lemon juice
2 teaspoons soy sauce

Heat the oil in a non-stick frying pan over high heat. Add the rice, ginger, chilli and onion and cook stirring for 5 minutes or until the rice is slightly crisp.

Add the crab meat and the eggs. Stir for 30 seconds to distribute the eggs. Reduce heat to low, cover and cook for 4–5 minutes or until the egg is set. Cut into wedges and divide between plates. Combine the coriander, snow peas, lemon and soy and serve with the omelette. SERVES 4.

+ You can buy fresh or frozen picked crab meat from your fishmonger.

thai rice with chilli salmon

2 cups (400g) jasmine rice
8 kaffir lime leaves*, shredded
¼ cup shredded ginger
2 long red chillies*, chopped
2½ cups (625ml) chicken stock
1 cup (250ml) water
chilli salmon
4 x 200g salmon fillets, skin on
2 tablespoons vegetable oil
2 teaspoons dried chilli flakes
lime wedges, to serve

Place the rice, lime leaf, ginger, chilli, stock and water in a saucepan over medium heat and bring to the boil. Cook for 5 minutes, reduce heat to low, cover, and cook for 3 minutes. Remove rice from the heat and allow to stand, covered, for 5 minutes.

While the rice is cooking, make the chilli salmon. Cut each salmon fillet lengthways into 3 pieces. Heat half the oil in a large non-stick frying pan over high heat. Sprinkle the salmon with chilli flakes and cook half the salmon for 1 minute each side. Set aside and repeat with remaining oil and salmon. Divide the rice between plates, top with the salmon and serve with lime wedges. SERVES 4.

rice noodles with chilli cashews

375g dried rice noodles*
2 Lebanese cucumbers, thinly sliced
2 green mangoes*, peeled and thinly sliced
1 cup mint leaves
1 cup coriander (cilantro) leaves
½ cup (125ml) lime juice
¼ cup (60ml) fish sauce*
⅓ cup (75g) caster (superfine) sugar
chilli cashews
1¾ cups (270g) unsalted raw cashews, roughly chopped
1½ tablespoons fish sauce*
⅓ cup (45g) brown sugar
1 teaspoon dried chilli flakes
2 kaffir lime leaves*, finely chopped

Preheat oven to 180°C (350°F). To make the cashews, combine the nuts, fish sauce, sugar, chilli and lime leaf on a baking tray lined with non-stick baking paper. Bake for 10 minutes, stir, bake for a further 5 minutes, and cool. Cook noodles according to packet instructions and combine with the cucumber, mango, mint and coriander.

Combine the lime, fish sauce and sugar and pour over the noodles. Divide between plates and top with the nuts to serve. SERVES 4.

lemongrass chicken with noodle pancakes

2 tablespoons vegetable oil, plus extra, for frying
2 stalks lemongrass*, trimmed and very finely chopped
6 kaffir lime leaves*, very finely chopped
400g chicken mince (ground chicken)
2 tablespoons fish sauce*
1 tablespoon lime juice
100g dried rice vermicelli noodles*
1 tablespoon grated ginger
3 green onions (scallions), finely chopped
1 teaspoon dried chilli flakes
1 egg
mint leaves and bean sprouts, to serve

Heat the oil in non-stick frying pan over high heat, add the lemongrass and lime leaf and cook, stirring, for 2 minutes. Add the chicken and cook, stirring, for 5 minutes or until cooked through. Stir through fish sauce and lime and set aside. Cook the noodles according to packet instructions and combine with the ginger, onion, chilli and egg. Heat 5mm oil in a non-stick frying pan over medium heat. Drop 2 tablespoonfuls of the noodle mixture into the oil and cook, in batches, for 2–3 minutes each side. To serve, divide between plates, top with the chicken, mint and bean sprouts. SERVES 4.

I love the spicy coating on
the tofu and how it's perfectly
balanced with the soy noodles.

chilli salt and pepper tofu with soy noodles

pork meatballs with chinese noodles

chilli salt and pepper tofu with soy noodles

1 teaspoon dried chilli flakes
1 teaspoon Chinese five-spice powder*
1 teaspoon each table salt and cracked black pepper
2 tablespoons rice flour
800g firm tofu, sliced and patted dry
vegetable oil, for shallow frying
4 green onions (scallions), trimmed and sliced
soy noodles
450g udon noodles*
½ cup (125ml) soy sauce
⅓ cup (80ml) lemon juice
2 tablespoons caster (superfine) sugar
2 tablespoons toasted sesame seeds

To make the soy noodles, cook the noodles according to packet instructions. Combine the soy, lemon juice, sugar and sesame and pour over the noodles. Set aside.

Combine the chilli, five-spice, salt, pepper and flour. Press the tofu slices evenly in the spice mixture to coat. Heat 5mm of oil in a frying pan over medium–low heat. Add the tofu, in batches, and cook for 1–2 minutes each side or until golden. Drain on absorbent paper. Divide the noodles between plates and top with the tofu and green onion to serve. SERVES 4.

pork meatballs with chinese noodles

450g fresh egg noodles or Singapore noodles*
500g pork mince (ground pork)
¼ cup (15g) fresh breadcrumbs
2 tablespoons finely grated ginger
¼ cup (60ml) hoisin sauce
½ cup (75g) sesame seeds
2 tablespoons vegetable oil
1 teaspoon sesame oil
3 cloves garlic, sliced
3 long red chillies*, seeds removed and sliced
¼ cup (60ml) oyster sauce
¼ cup (60ml) chicken stock
½ cup coriander (cilantro) leaves

Cook the noodles according to packet instructions and set aside. Place the pork, breadcrumbs, ginger and hoisin in a bowl and mix to combine. Shape tablespoonfuls of mixture into balls and roll in sesame. Heat the oil in a non-stick frying pan over medium heat. Add the meatballs and cook for 6–8 minutes each side or until cooked through. Set aside. Wipe out the pan with absorbent paper and add the sesame oil, garlic and chilli and cook for 2 minutes. Add the noodles, oyster sauce, stock and meatballs and toss to heat through. Divide between bowls and top with coriander to serve. SERVES 4.

simple paella

1 red onion, sliced
1 teaspoon dried chilli flakes
1 teaspoon smoked paprika*
3 chorizo*, sliced
4 x 125g chicken thigh fillets, trimmed and chopped
1¼ cups (250g) short-grain rice
1 litre (4 cups) chicken stock
12 green (raw) king prawns (shrimp), peeled with tails intact
¾ cup coriander (cilantro) leaves
250g cherry tomatoes, quartered
lemon wedges, to serve

Heat a large, deep non-stick frying pan over high heat. Add the onion, chilli, paprika and chorizo and cook for 3–5 minutes or until golden. Add the chicken and cook, turning, for 3 minutes or until sealed. Add the rice and stir until coated. Add the stock, bring to the boil and cook for 10 minutes. Add the prawns and cook for a further 5 minutes or until the rice is tender. Divide between plates, and top with coriander and tomatoes and serve with lemon wedges. SERVES 4.

baked chicken and porcini risotto

25g dried porcini mushrooms*
¾ cup (180ml) boiling water
4 x 125g chicken thigh fillets, trimmed and chopped
2 cups (400g) arborio (risotto) rice
1 litre (4 cups) chicken stock
2 teaspoons thyme leaves
1 clove garlic, crushed
50g butter, chopped
1 cup (80g) finely grated parmesan
sea salt and cracked black pepper
finely grated parmesan, extra, to serve

Preheat oven to 200°C (400°F). Place the mushrooms in a bowl and cover with the boiling water. Allow to stand for 5 minutes. Drain the mushrooms, reserving the soaking liquid. Chop the mushrooms and place in a 3-litre capacity ovenproof dish with the mushroom soaking water, chicken, rice, stock, thyme and garlic. Stir to combine, cover tightly with aluminium foil and bake for 35–40 minutes. Remove from the oven, add the butter, parmesan, salt and pepper and stir for 3–4 minutes or until the risotto thickens. Divide between bowls and top with the parmesan to serve. SERVES 4.

This cheat's version of paella
takes next to no time to cook
and has the same robust flavour.

simple paella

This is my favourite no-stir risotto. The porcini gives it a deep, earthy flavour.

baked chicken and porcini risotto

tips & tricks

RIGHT
Rice noodles are great
for salads and soups,
as are vermicelli,
while wheat and egg
noodles are suited to
speedy stir-frying.

BELOW
For the best results
with rice, I prefer the
absorption method.
As a rule of thumb,
use $1\frac{1}{2}$ cups of water
to 1 cup of rice.

Versatile noodles and
rice are the perfect
blank canvas for
many flavours and are
excellent standbys for
any night of the week.

ABOVE
Short-grain rice is
starchy and best for
paella or rice pudding.
Long-grain rice is a
great basic side, while
arborio is the rice to
choose for risotto.

LEFT
To measure servings,
the best guide is that
1 cup of uncooked rice
will yield 3 cups of
cooked rice.

couscous, beans & lentils

butter bean, green olive and white anchovy salad

spicy one-pot couscous

butter bean, green olive and white anchovy salad

2 cups (140g) fresh breadcrumbs
2 tablespoons olive oil
2 tablespoons salted capers, rinsed
½ cup (40g) finely grated parmesan
2 x 400g cans butter beans, drained and rinsed
½ cup (60g) chopped green olives
12 white anchovy fillets*
½ cup flat-leaf parsley leaves
1 cup mache lettuce leaves
sea salt and cracked black pepper
lemon juice and olive oil, to serve

Preheat oven to 180°C (350°F). Place the breadcrumbs, oil, capers and parmesan in a bowl and toss well to combine. Place on a baking tray lined with non-stick baking paper and bake for 15 minutes. Stir the crumbs and bake for a further 10 minutes or until golden.

Place the beans, olives, anchovy, parsley, lettuce, salt and pepper in a bowl and toss to combine. Divide between plates, drizzle with lemon juice and olive oil and top with the crispy parmesan crumbs to serve. SERVES 4.

spicy one-pot couscous

2 teaspoons olive oil
2 red onions, cut into fine wedges
4 chorizo*, sliced
½ teaspoon dried chilli flakes
2 teaspoons rosemary leaves
2 cups (400g) instant couscous
2¾ cups (680ml) chicken stock
150g baby spinach leaves
½ cup flat-leaf parsley leaves
lemon wedges and store-bought aïoli*, to serve

Heat the oil in a deep non-stick frying pan over medium–high heat. Add the onion, chorizo, chilli and rosemary and cook for 7–9 minutes or until the chorizo and onions are golden. Add the couscous and chicken stock. Reduce heat to low, cover and simmer for 7–8 minutes or until the stock is absorbed. Stir through the spinach and parsley. Spoon into bowls and serve with lemon wedges and aïoli. SERVES 4.

chickpea, feta and carrot fritters

2 x 440g can chickpeas (garbanzos), drained and rinsed
4 carrots, peeled and grated
1 cup chopped coriander (cilantro) leaves
300g firm feta, chopped
4 eggs
½ cup (100g) rice flour
2 teaspoons baking powder
sea salt and cracked black pepper
vegetable oil, for shallow frying
lemon wedges, minted yoghurt and baby spinach leaves, to serve

Place the chickpeas in a bowl and roughly mash with a fork. Add the carrot, coriander and feta and mix to combine. Add the eggs, rice flour, baking powder, salt and pepper and mix well.

Heat 1cm of oil in a large frying pan over medium heat. Add large spoonfuls of the mixture to the pan and cook, in batches, for 2–3 minutes each side or until golden. Drain on absorbent paper. Serve the warm fritters with lemon wedges, minted yoghurt, and baby spinach leaves. SERVES 4.

Nutty chickpeas, sweet carrot and tangy feta combine in these tasty vegetable fritters. I dare you to try stopping at just one.

chickpea, feta and carrot fritters

preserved lemon, lentil and fried tomato salad

2 x 400g cans green lentils, drained and rinsed
2 tablespoons shredded preserved lemon rind*
1 tablespoon red wine vinegar
2 tablespoons olive oil, plus extra, for drizzling
sea salt and cracked black pepper
6 vine-ripened tomatoes, thickly sliced
40g butter, melted
2 tablespoons white sugar
100g baby rocket (arugula) leaves
½ cup flat-leaf parsley leaves, roughly chopped
125g goat's curd*, to serve

Place the lentils, lemon rind, vinegar, oil, salt and pepper in a bowl and set aside to marinate for 15 minutes.

Heat a non-stick frying pan over high heat. Brush both sides of the tomatoes with butter and sprinkle with sugar. Cook the tomatoes, in batches, for 2–3 minutes each side or until golden.

Toss the rocket and parsley with the lentils and divide between plates. Top with the fried tomatoes and a spoonful of goat's curd and drizzle with extra olive oil, to serve. SERVES 4.

smashed chickpea salad with chorizo

1 x 400g can chickpeas (garbanzos), drained and rinsed
½ red onion, finely chopped
1 cup flat-leaf parsley leaves
sea salt and cracked black pepper
⅓ cup (80ml) lemon juice
2 tablespoons tahini*
2 tablespoons olive oil
4 chorizo*, sliced
lemon wedges, to serve

Place the chickpeas in a bowl and roughly mash with a fork. Toss with the onion, parsley, salt and pepper. Place the lemon juice, tahini and oil in a bowl and whisk to combine. Pour the dressing over the salad and allow to marinate for 5 minutes.

Cook the chorizo under a preheated hot grill (broiler) for 3–4 minutes each side or until golden. Divide the chickpea salad between plates and top with the chorizo and lemon wedges to serve. SERVES 4.

prawn and white bean salad

20 cooked prawns (shrimp), peeled with tails intact
1 x 400g can white (cannellini) beans, drained and rinsed
1 butter lettuce, cut into wedges
1 avocado, cut into wedges
lime wedges, to serve
coriander and lime dressing
½ cup coriander (cilantro) leaves
1 long green chilli*, chopped
2 tablespoons lime juice
1 tablespoon vegetable oil
1 tablespoon caster (superfine) sugar

To make the coriander and lime dressing, place the coriander, chilli, lime juice, oil and sugar in a small food processor and process until finely chopped. Place the prawns and beans in a bowl and pour over the dressing to marinate for 10 minutes. Divide the lettuce and avocado between plates and top with the prawn, beans and dressing. Serve with lime wedges. SERVES 4.

porcini, bacon and maple beans

20g dried porcini mushrooms*
1 cup (250ml) boiling water
1 tablespoon olive oil
1 leek, trimmed and sliced
4 rashers bacon, trimmed and chopped
1 cup (250ml) chicken stock
2 x 400g cans borlotti beans, drained and rinsed
1 tablespoon maple syrup
sea salt and cracked black pepper
flat-leaf parsley leaves and hot buttered toast, to serve

Place the porcini in a bowl and cover with the boiling water. Allow to stand for 8 minutes. Drain the porcini, reserving the soaking liquid, slice and set aside.

Heat the oil in a non-stick frying pan over medium heat. Add the leek and bacon and cook for 8 minutes or until golden. Add the porcini, stock and beans and simmer for 6 minutes or until the sauce has reduced. Stir through the maple syrup, salt and pepper. Sprinkle with parsley and serve with hot buttered toast. SERVES 4.

This twice-cooked chicken is
first poached then fried, making
it tender, juicy and super crispy.

crispy chicken with almond couscous

lentil and sausage cassoulet

crispy chicken with almond couscous

3 cups (750ml) chicken stock
4 large pieces lemon rind
8 sprigs thyme
1 x 1.6kg chicken, cut into 8 pieces
1¼ cups (250g) instant couscous
¾ cup (150g) rice flour
2 tablespoons sumac*
sea salt and cracked black pepper
vegetable oil, for shallow frying
½ cup (70g) slivered almonds, toasted
2 tablespoons chopped flat-leaf parsley leaves
lemon wedges, extra sumac* and harissa*, to serve

Place the stock, lemon rind and thyme in a large deep frying pan over medium heat and bring to the boil. Add the chicken and simmer for 8 minutes each side+. Remove from the pan and place on a wire rack. Remove the lemon and thyme from the pan and discard. Remove 1½ cups (375ml) of the hot stock and pour into a bowl. Add the couscous, cover and set aside.

   Combine the rice flour, sumac and a generous sprinkling of salt and pepper. Dust the chicken with the flour mixture, shaking off any excess. Heat 1cm of oil in a frying pan over high heat and shallow fry the chicken for 2–3 minutes each side or until golden. Drain on absorbent paper.

   Stir the almonds and parsley through the couscous and divide the couscous and chicken between plates. Serve with lemon wedges, a sprinkling of extra sumac and harissa. SERVES 4.
+ You may need to cook the thicker thigh pieces for 2 minutes longer.

lentil and sausage cassoulet

6 pork sausages
1 tablespoon olive oil
2 leeks, trimmed and sliced
2 tablespoons oregano leaves
1 x 120g piece flat pancetta*, chopped
2 cups (500ml) chicken stock
1 x 400g can green lentils, drained and rinsed
flat-leaf parsley leaves and lemon wedges, to serve

Heat a non-stick frying pan over medium heat. Add the sausages and cook for 3 minutes each side or until cooked through. Set aside. Add the oil, leeks, oregano and pancetta to the pan and cook for 5 minutes or until the leeks are soft and golden. Add the stock, bring to the boil and simmer for 5 minutes. Slice the sausages and return to the pan with the lentils. Simmer for 4 minutes or until warmed through. Divide between bowls and serve with parsley and lemon wedges. SERVES 4.

spicy lamb meatball and lentil soup

375g lamb mince (ground lamb)
2 tablespoons harissa*
1 teaspoon smoked paprika*
½ cup (35g) fresh breadcrumbs
1 egg
2 teaspoons olive oil
1 brown onion, sliced
3 cloves garlic, sliced
1.25 litres (5 cups) chicken stock
1 cup (200g) dried red lentils
2 cups (100g) English spinach leaves
sea salt and cracked black pepper
thick natural yoghurt, to serve

To make the meatballs, place the lamb, harissa, paprika, breadcrumbs and egg in a bowl and mix very well to combine. Roll tablespoonfuls of the mixture into meatballs and set aside.

   Heat the oil in a saucepan over medium heat. Add the onion and garlic and cook for 5 minutes or until soft. Add the stock and bring to a rapid simmer. Add the lentils, cover, and cook for 7 minutes or until the lentils are starting to soften. Add the meatballs and cook for a further 5–7 minutes or until they are cooked through. Stir through the spinach, salt and pepper. Ladle the soup into bowls and top with the yoghurt to serve. SERVES 4.

chicken, chilli and lemon couscous soup

2 teaspoons olive oil
1 teaspoon dried chilli flakes
1 tablespoon finely grated lemon rind
1 brown onion, sliced
1.5 litres (6 cups) chicken stock
3 x 200g chicken breast fillets, trimmed and thinly sliced
100g green beans, trimmed and chopped
¾ cup (150g) instant couscous
coriander (cilantro) leaves, to serve

Heat the oil in a large saucepan over medium–high heat. Add the chilli, lemon and onion and cook for 4 minutes or until the onion is soft. Add the stock and bring to a simmer. Add the chicken and cook, stirring, for 2 minutes. Add the beans and couscous and cook, stirring occasionally, for 3–4 minutes or until the couscous is soft. Spoon into bowls and top with coriander to serve. SERVES 4.

This generous warming soup
is a complete meal and sure to
satisfy – I call it my man soup.

spicy lamb meatball and lentil soup

chicken, chilli and lemon couscous soup

tips & tricks

RIGHT
Couscous is a great vehicle for flavour. Try adding grated lemon rind for a zesty kick and fresh herbs such as coriander and mint.

BELOW
Canned beans and chickpeas can be a little starchy at times, so it's best to drain and rinse them before using in cooking.

Cans of beans, chickpeas and lentils are lifesavers in the kitchen. They can become easy salads and sides and add substance to soups.

ABOVE
For instant couscous, the liquid to couscous ratio is usually 1:1, which should yield a fluffy result. Use stock instead of water for more flavour.

LEFT
You can freeze cooked couscous and rice in air-tight containers to use later in salads, sides or stuffings.

chicken

spiced yoghurt grilled chicken skewers

roasted chicken with pancetta and lentils

spiced yoghurt grilled chicken skewers

¼ cup finely chopped coriander (cilantro) leaves
¼ cup finely chopped flat-leaf parsley leaves
1 clove garlic, crushed
1 teaspoon smoked paprika*
1 teaspoon ground cumin
2 teaspoons finely grated lemon rind
1 cup (280g) thick plain yoghurt
6 x 125g chicken thigh fillets, trimmed and quartered
warm flat bread*, mache lettuce and store-bought hummus,
   to serve

Place the coriander, parsley, garlic, paprika, cumin, lemon rind and
yoghurt in a bowl and mix to combine. Thread 3 pieces of chicken
onto each skewer and coat generously in the spiced yoghurt.
Set aside for 10 minutes to marinate. Preheat a grill (broiler) on
high heat. Place the skewers on a wire rack on a baking tray and
grill (broil) for 6–7 minutes each side or until golden and cooked
through. Serve the chicken skewers with warm flat bread, lettuce,
hummus and a tomato and mint salad, if desired. SERVES 4.

roasted chicken with pancetta and lentils

vegetable oil, for frying
8 x 200g chicken thighs, bone in, skin on, trimmed
sea salt and cracked black pepper
2 leeks, trimmed and thinly sliced
1 x 150g piece flat pancetta*, chopped
2 sprigs rosemary
1 x 400g can green lentils, drained and rinsed
250g cherry tomatoes
1 cup (250ml) chicken stock
½ cup flat-leaf parsley leaves

Preheat oven to 200°C (400°F). Heat a little oil in an ovenproof
frying pan over high heat. Sprinkle the chicken with salt and pepper,
add to the pan, skin-side down, and cook for 7 minutes each side
or until well browned. Remove from the pan and set aside.
   Add the leeks, pancetta and rosemary to the pan and cook for
4–5 minutes or until golden. Stir through the lentils, tomatoes
and stock and return the chicken to the pan. Place in the oven and
roast for 12 minutes or until chicken is golden and cooked through.
Stir through the parsley to serve. SERVES 4.

spice-baked chicken with tzatziki salad

1 teaspoon ground cumin
½ teaspoon dried chilli flakes
1 tablespoon thyme leaves
1 tablespoon shredded lemon zest
1 tablespoon olive oil
4 x 200g chicken breast fillets, trimmed
tzatziki salad
½ cup (140g) thick plain yoghurt
2 tablespoons lemon juice
sea salt
4 cucumbers, sliced lengthways with a vegetable peeler
1 cup mint leaves
½ cup chopped dill leaves

Preheat oven to 200°C (400°F). Place the cumin, chilli, thyme,
lemon zest and oil in a large bowl and mix to combine. Add the
chicken and toss to coat. Place the chicken in a baking dish lined
with non-stick baking paper and roast for 15 minutes or until
chicken is just cooked through.
   While the chicken is cooking, make the tzatziki salad. Place the
yoghurt, lemon juice and salt in a bowl and mix to combine. Divide
the cucumber, mint and dill between plates and spoon over the
dressing. Slice the chicken and serve with the salad. SERVES 4.

I've borrowed the traditional
ingredients of a cooling tzatziki
and turned them into a refreshing
salad for this spicy chicken.

spice-baked chicken with tzatziki salad

chicken pan pie

1 tablespoon olive oil
1 large brown onion, chopped
8 x 150g chicken thigh fillets, trimmed and chopped
2 tablespoons plain (all-purpose) flour
400g button mushrooms, halved
¾ cup (180ml) chicken stock
¾ cup (180ml) single (pouring) cream*
2 tablespoons lemon juice
1 tablespoon chopped tarragon
sea salt and cracked black pepper
2 sheets store-bought puff pastry, thawed

Preheat oven to 200°C (400°F). Heat the oil in a deep ovenproof frying pan over high heat. Add the onion and cook for 2–3 minutes or until golden. Dust the chicken with flour, add to the pan and cook, turning, for 6 minutes or until well browned. Add the mushrooms and cook for 2 minutes. Add the stock, cream, lemon juice, tarragon, salt and pepper and simmer for 20 minutes or until chicken is cooked through and sauce has reduced. Cut a round of pastry to fit inside the rim of the frying pan, or use 4 x 2-cup capacity (500ml) ramekins. Place the pastry on top of the chicken, transfer pan to the oven and bake for 20 minutes or until pastry is puffed and golden. SERVES 4.

fast garlic chicken

60g butter, softened
4 cloves garlic, crushed
sea salt flakes
1 x 1.6kg whole chicken
8 large sprigs rosemary
olive oil, for drizzling

Preheat oven to 200°C (400°F). Place the butter, garlic and salt in a small bowl and mix to combine. Using kitchen scissors, cut down the backbone of the chicken and remove the backbone. Press firmly on the breastbone to flatten. Gently loosen the skin from the flesh using your fingers and push the garlic butter under.

Place the rosemary in a baking dish lined with non-stick baking paper and top with the chicken. Drizzle with a little oil and sprinkle with extra sea salt. Roast for 40 minutes or until the chicken is cooked through. Cut into quarters and serve with a simple salad or crispy oven chips, if desired. SERVES 4.

chicken spoon dumpling soup

375g dried rice noodles*
350g chicken mince (ground chicken)
1 tablespoon finely grated ginger
2 green onions (scallions), finely chopped
2 tablespoons hoisin sauce
1.5 litres (6 cups) chicken stock
½ cup (125ml) Chinese cooking wine* (Shaoxing) or dry sherry
6 slices ginger, extra
2 tablespoons hoisin sauce, extra
8 stalks gai larn*
sliced green onion (scallion), extra, to serve

Cook the noodles according to packet instructions, drain and set aside. Place the chicken mince, ginger, onions and hoisin in a bowl and mix well to combine. Set aside.

Place the chicken stock, wine, extra ginger and hoisin in a large deep frying pan and bring to the boil. Drop spoonfuls of the chicken mixture into the simmering soup. Cook the dumplings for 2 minutes, add the gai larn and cook for a further 1–2 minutes.

Divide the noodles between bowls and top with the dumplings, gai larn, soup and extra green onions to serve. SERVES 4.

almond roasted chicken

½ teaspoon ground cumin
1 tablespoon shredded lemon zest
1 tablespoon lemon juice
1 tablespoon olive oil
½ teaspoon ground cinnamon
sea salt and cracked black pepper
4 x 200g chicken breast fillets, trimmed
½ cup (80g) blanched whole almonds
2 tablespoons currants
8 sprigs oregano

Preheat oven to 200°C (400°F). Place the cumin, lemon zest and juice, oil, cinnamon, salt and pepper in a large bowl and mix to combine. Add the chicken and toss to coat. Place the chicken in a baking dish lined with non-stick baking paper. Sprinkle the almonds, currants and oregano over the chicken. Roast for 14–18 minutes or until chicken is just cooked through. Serve the chicken with a simple feta and mint salad, if desired. SERVES 4.

grilled chicken salad with green chilli ranch dressing

With its creamy coconut dressing and crunchy vegetables, this is a great Asian take on the classic.

asian chicken slaw

grilled chicken salad with green chilli ranch dressing

4 x 200g chicken breast fillets, trimmed and thickly sliced
olive oil, for brushing
1 teaspoon smoked paprika*
1 teaspoon ground coriander (cilantro)
sea salt and cracked black pepper
4 corn tortillas
2 baby cos (romaine) or iceberg lettuces, halved
shaved manchego* cheese, to serve
green chilli ranch dressing
4 long green chillies*, seeds removed, chopped
½ cup (125ml) buttermilk
½ cup (120g) sour cream
1 tablespoon lemon juice

To make the ranch dressing, place the chilli, buttermilk, sour cream and lemon juice in small bowl and stir to combine. Set aside.

Brush the chicken with a little oil and sprinkle with the combined paprika, coriander, salt and pepper. Heat a char-grill pan or barbecue over high heat and cook the chicken for 2–3 minutes each side or until cooked through. Cut the tortillas into thick strips, brush with a little oil and char-grill until golden and crisp.

Divide the lettuce, chicken, tortillas and manchego between plates and spoon over the ranch dressing to serve. SERVES 4.

asian chicken slaw

6 cups shredded Chinese cabbage (wombok)
2 carrots, shredded lengthways
1 cup (150g) roasted unsalted cashews
¼ cup snipped chives
1 cup mint leaves
1 cup coriander (cilantro) leaves
2 long red chillies*, seeds removed, finely sliced
4 x 200g cooked chicken breasts, shredded
lime and coconut dressing
½ cup (125ml) coconut milk
1 tablespoon fish sauce*
2 tablespoons lime juice
1 tablespoon caster (superfine) sugar

Place the cabbage, carrot, cashews, chives, mint, coriander, chilli and chicken in a bowl and toss to combine.

To make the lime and coconut dressing, place the coconut milk, fish sauce, lime juice and sugar in a bowl and whisk to combine. Pour the dressing over the salad and toss gently to combine. Divide between plates to serve. SERVES 4.

thai poached chicken

¾ cup (180ml) chicken stock
2 tablespoons fish sauce*
⅓ cup (80ml) lime juice
1 long red chilli*, seeds removed and finely sliced
6 kaffir lime leaves*, shredded
¼ cup (55g) brown sugar or grated palm sugar*
4 x 200g chicken breast fillets, trimmed
steamed jasmine rice and coriander (cilantro) leaves, to serve

Place the stock, fish sauce, lime juice, chilli, lime leaf and sugar in a non-stick frying pan over medium–high heat and bring to the boil. Reduce heat and simmer for 3 minutes. Add the chicken and cook for 7–9 minutes each side or until cooked through. Divide between plates, top with poaching liquid and serve with steamed jasmine rice and coriander. SERVES 4.

stir-fried salt and pepper chicken with coriander noodles

375g dried rice noodles*
2 tablespoons vegetable oil
2 teaspoons sea salt flakes
2 teaspoons Chinese five-spice powder*
2 teaspoons dried chilli flakes
1 teaspoon cracked black pepper
4 x 200g chicken breast fillets, trimmed and sliced
½ cup (100g) rice flour
2 tablespoons soy sauce
⅓ cup (80ml) lemon juice
1 cup coriander (cilantro) leaves
360g broccolini (sprouting broccoli), blanched
2 green onions (scallions), sliced

Cook the rice noodles according to packet instructions, drain and set aside. Heat a large non-stick frying pan over high heat. Add the oil, salt, five-spice, chilli and pepper and cook for 1 minute or until fragrant. Toss the chicken in the rice flour, shaking off any excess, add to the pan and cook, in batches, for 2 minutes each side or until golden and cooked through.

Place the noodles in a bowl with the soy, lemon juice, coriander, broccolini and green onions and toss to combine. Divide the noodles between bowls and top with the chicken to serve. SERVES 4.

thai poached chicken

stir-fried salt and pepper chicken with coriander noodles

tips & tricks

Chicken works well with the fresh and zesty flavour of lemon as well as robust garlic and with fragrant herbs such tarragon or thyme.

For lovely succulent chicken breast, brown the meat in a hot frying pan on both sides, reduce heat to low, cover, and cook for 2–3 minutes.

Chicken is one of the most versatile ingredients and lends itself to many cooking techniques as well as a world of cuisines and flavours.

ABOVE

To check when a roasted chicken is perfectly cooked, pierce the flesh under the thigh with a skewer. It's ready when the juice runs clear, not pink.

LEFT

Breast isn't necessarily always best. It's great for poaching and shredding into salads, say, but for barbecuing, the darker thigh meat is the juiciest cut.

beef

They don't call these minute
steaks for nothing. This is the
fastest flavour-packed dinner yet.

parmesan minute steaks with garlic spinach

sage salt steak with pancetta-baked polenta

parmesan minute steaks with garlic spinach

3 cups (240g) finely grated parmesan
cracked black pepper
8 x 100g thin beef minute steaks
vegetable oil, for frying
45g butter
6 cloves garlic, sliced
1 tablespoon finely grated lemon rind
200g baby spinach leaves
sea salt and cracked black pepper

Combine the parmesan and pepper and place in a flat shallow dish. Press both sides of the steaks firmly into the parmesan mixture. Heat the oil in a large non-stick frying pan over high heat and cook the steaks, in batches, for 30 seconds each side or until browned. Divide between warmed plates.

Wipe out the pan with absorbent paper and add the butter, garlic and lemon rind and cook until the garlic is golden. Add the spinach, salt and pepper and toss until wilted. Serve the steaks with the garlic spinach and potato chips, if desired. SERVES 4.

sage salt steak with pancetta-baked polenta

1 teaspoon mustard powder
1 tablespoon sea salt flakes
2 tablespoons very finely chopped sage leaves
4 x 250g T-bone steaks, trimmed
pancetta-baked polenta
2 cups (500ml) chicken stock
1 cup (250ml) milk
¾ cup (120g) instant polenta
½ cup (40g) finely grated parmesan
⅓ cup shredded basil leaves
30g butter
sea salt and cracked black pepper
12 slices round pancetta*

Preheat oven to 180°C (350°F). To make the pancetta-baked polenta, heat the stock and milk in a saucepan over medium heat until boiling. Whisk in the polenta and stir for 2–3 minutes or until smooth. Remove from the heat and stir through the parmesan, basil, butter, salt and pepper. Line the bases and sides of a 4 x greased 1-cup (250ml) capacity non-stick muffin tin or ramekins with the pancetta. Spoon in the polenta and bake for 25 minutes or until golden.

Mix to combine the mustard powder, salt and sage. Sprinkle the sage salt over the steaks and cook on a barbecue or in a non-stick frying pan over medium–high heat for 5 minutes for medium or until cooked to your liking. Divide the steaks between plates and serve with remaining sage salt and the pancetta-baked polenta. SERVES 4.

tomato, olive and mozzarella meatballs

2 cups (140g) fresh breadcrumbs
⅓ cup (80ml) milk
750g beef mince (ground beef)
⅓ cup (90g) store-bought basil pesto
⅓ cup chopped flat-leaf parsley leaves
sea salt and cracked black pepper
2 tablespoons olive oil
500g cherry tomatoes, seeds removed
¼ cup small oregano sprigs
1 cup (150g) green Sicilian olives
200g baby bocconcini*
1 cup basil leaves and crusty bread, to serve

Place the breadcrumbs in a bowl, pour over the milk and stand until the milk has absorbed. Place the mince, pesto, breadcrumb mixture, parsley, salt and pepper in a bowl and mix well to combine. Beat the mixture with a spatula for 2 minutes until smooth. Roll ¼ cupfuls of the mixture into meatballs.

Preheat oven to 200°C (400°F). Heat the oil in a non-stick frying pan over medium heat and cook the meatballs, in batches, for 2 minutes each side or until golden but not cooked through. Transfer the meatballs to a baking dish with the cherry tomatoes, oregano, olives and bocconcini. Bake for 20 minutes or until the bocconcini are melted and the meatballs are cooked through. Sprinkle with basil leaves and serve with crusty bread. SERVES 4.

Kids big and small will love these meatballs, covered in molten mozzarella and sweet tomatoes.

tomato, olive and mozzarella meatballs

shaved beef and celery salad with bloody mary dressing

500g beef fillet, trimmed
sea salt and cracked black pepper
1 celery heart, trimmed
3 stalks celery, trimmed
1 cup small celery leaves
bloody mary dressing
½ cup (125ml) tomato juice
1 tablespoon vodka
½ teaspoon Tabasco sauce
1 teaspoon Worcestershire sauce

Preheat oven to 200°C (400°F). Heat a non-stick frying pan over high heat. Sprinkle the beef with salt and pepper and cook for 3 minutes each side or until well browned. Transfer the beef to a baking tray and roast for 15–20 minutes for medium or until cooked to your liking. Rest for 5 minutes, thinly slice and set aside.

Using a mandolin, thinly slice the celery heart and stalks and toss with the celery leaves. Divide between plates and top with the sliced beef. To make the bloody mary dressing, whisk together the tomato juice, vodka, Tabasco, Worcestershire, salt and pepper. Spoon over the salad and serve with thin potato chips, if desired. SERVES 4.

mustard steaks with horseradish rösti

4 x 200g rump steaks, trimmed
sea salt and cracked black pepper
2 cups watercress sprigs
¼ cup (60ml) Dijon mustard
¼ cup (70g) sour cream
horseradish rösti
3 starchy potatoes, peeled and grated
⅓ cup (70g) store-bought grated horseradish*
1 cup (80g) finely grated parmesan
75g butter, melted

To make the horseradish rösti, place the potato, horseradish, parmesan, butter, salt and pepper in a bowl and mix to combine. Heat a non-stick frying pan over medium heat and add enough potato mixture to thinly coat the bottom of the pan. Cook for 6 minutes each side or until golden. Repeat with remaining mixture and keep in a warm oven until ready to serve.

Sprinkle the steaks with salt and pepper and cook on a preheated barbecue or char-grill pan over high heat for 2 minutes each side for medium or until cooked to your liking. Rest for 2 minutes and thickly slice. Divide rösti between plates and top with steak, watercress and spoonfuls of combined mustard and sour cream to serve. SERVES 4.

thyme-crumbed veal cutlets

4 cups (280g) fresh breadcrumbs
3 tablespoons thyme leaves
2 tablespoons finely grated lemon rind
3 cloves garlic, crushed
sea salt and cracked black pepper
1 egg, lightly beaten
2 tablespoons Dijon mustard
4 x 125g veal cutlets, pounded until ½ cm thick
vegetable oil, for shallow frying
lemon wedges, to serve

Place the breadcrumbs, thyme, lemon rind, garlic, salt and pepper
in a wide bowl and mix to combine. Place the egg and mustard in a
shallow dish and whisk to combine. Dip the veal cutlets in the egg
mixture and press into the breadcrumb mixture.

Heat 1cm of oil in a large non-stick frying pan over medium–high
heat. Add the cutlets and cook, in batches, for 2–3 minutes each
side or until golden. Keep the cutlets in a warm oven until ready to
serve. Serve the cutlets with lemon wedges and a shaved fennel and
radicchio salad, if desired. SERVES 4.

prosciutto-wrapped steaks with mushroom and leek tarts

1 sheet store-bought puff pastry, thawed
1 leek, trimmed and sliced
16 sprigs thyme
60g butter, melted
4 small field mushrooms
4 x 180g scotch or eye fillet steaks, trimmed
4 slices prosciutto
sea salt and cracked black pepper
mustard, to serve

Preheat oven to 200°C (400°F). Cut the pastry into 4 squares
and place on a baking tray lined with non-stick baking paper. Divide
the leek and thyme between the squares and brush with a little
butter. Top with mushrooms and brush with more butter. Bake for
20 minutes or until puffed and golden.

While the tarts are baking, wrap the edge of each steak with
prosciutto and sprinkle with salt and pepper. Heat a non-stick frying
pan over medium–high heat, add the steaks and cook for 5 minutes
each side for medium or until cooked to your liking. Serve steaks with
the tarts, mustard and a baby spinach salad, if desired. SERVES 4.

spiced beef patties with crushed pea salad

italian veal and herb salad with crispy capers

spiced beef patties with crushed pea salad

1 tablespoon vegetable oil, plus extra, for frying
2 teaspoons cumin seeds
1 teaspoon dried chilli flakes
1 brown onion, finely chopped
1 cup (70g) fresh breadcrumbs
¼ cup (60ml) milk
600g beef mince (ground beef)
sea salt and cracked black pepper
labne* and flat bread, to serve
crushed pea salad
2 cups (300g) frozen peas
½ cup roughly chopped mint leaves
1 teaspoon finely grated lemon rind
1 tablespoon olive oil

Heat the oil in a non-stick frying pan over medium heat. Add the cumin, chilli and onion and cook, stirring, for 5 minutes or until onion is golden. Remove from pan and set aside. Place the breadcrumbs in a bowl, pour over the milk and stand until the milk has absorbed. Place the mince, breadcrumbs, salt, pepper and onion in a bowl and mix well to combine. Shape the mixture into 16 small 1cm thick patties. Heat a little oil in the frying pan over medium heat and cook the patties, in batches, for 2–3 minutes each side or until cooked through.

To make the crushed pea salad, cover the peas with boiling water for 2 minutes, drain and roughly mash with a fork. Combine the peas with the mint, lemon, oil, salt and pepper. Divide the patties between plates and serve with labne, flat bread and the pea salad. SERVES 4.

italian veal and herb salad with crispy capers

1 tablespoon chopped tarragon leaves
sea salt and cracked black pepper
500g boneless veal loin, trimmed
1 tablespoon olive oil
8 baby (new) potatoes, steamed and halved
1 cup flat-leaf parsley leaves
100g baby spinach leaves
¼ cup (50g) salted capers, rinsed and fried until crisp
creamy tuna dressing
½ cup (150g) whole-egg mayonnaise
2 tablespoons lemon juice
2 teaspoons Dijon mustard
1 x 95g can tuna, drained

Preheat oven to 180°C (350°F). Combine the tarragon, salt and pepper and sprinkle onto a sheet of non-stick baking paper. Roll the veal in the tarragon. Heat the oil in a non-stick frying pan over high heat, add the veal and cook for 4 minutes each side or until well browned. Transfer to a baking tray and roast for 8–10 minutes for medium-rare or until cooked to your liking. Rest for 5 minutes, slice

and set aside. To make the dressing, place the mayonnaise, lemon juice, mustard and tuna in a food processor and process until smooth. Divide the potatoes, parsley and spinach between plates and top with the veal. Spoon over the dressing and capers to serve. SERVES 4.

balsamic steaks with tomato and mint salad

¼ cup (60ml) balsamic vinegar
1 tablespoon brown sugar
2 teaspoons chopped rosemary leaves
1 tablespoon olive oil, plus extra, for brushing
sea salt and cracked black pepper
4 x 180g New York or porterhouse steaks, trimmed
4 thick slices haloumi*
tomato and mint salad
400g small mixed heirloom tomatoes, sliced
½ white onion, sliced
½ cup mint leaves
1 tablespoon olive oil, extra

Combine the vinegar, sugar, rosemary, oil, salt and pepper and pour over the steaks. Marinate for 10 minutes each side. While the steaks are marinating, make the tomato salad. Place the tomatoes, onion, mint, extra oil, salt and pepper in a bowl and toss to combine.

Heat a non-stick frying pan, barbecue or char-grill pan over medium–high heat and cook the steaks for 2 minutes each side or until cooked to your liking. Cover and set aside to rest.

Wipe out the pan with absorbent paper and place over medium heat. Brush the haloumi with oil and cook for 2 minutes each side or until golden. Divide the steaks between plates and top with the haloumi and the tomato and mint salad to serve. SERVES 4.

garlic pepper beef stir-fry

2 tablespoons vegetable oil
750g rump steak, trimmed and thinly sliced
2 teaspoons cracked black pepper
1 long red chilli*, sliced
4 cloves garlic, sliced
250g green beans, trimmed and halved
2 tablespoons oyster sauce
2 tablespoons beef or chicken stock
steamed jasmine rice and Thai basil leaves, to serve

Heat half the oil in a non-stick frying pan or wok over high heat. Add the beef and cook, in batches, for 4–5 minutes or until browned. Remove from the pan and set aside. Heat the remaining oil over high heat, add the pepper, chilli and garlic and cook for 1 minute or until fragrant. Return the beef to the pan with the green beans, oyster sauce and stock and cook, stirring, for 4 minutes or until warmed though. Serve with steamed rice and basil. SERVES 4.

balsamic steaks with tomato and mint salad

Sometimes simple is best.
Like this classic combination
of garlic and pepper with beef.

garlic pepper beef stir-fry

tips & tricks

RIGHT
Beef goes with classic flavour combinations of red wine, garlic and pepper, as well as a aromatic herbs such as tarragon.

BELOW
Steaks and cutlets are ideal for quick barbecuing or pan-frying, while chuck and blade steak are better suited to braising and slow cooking.

Whether it's a juicy steak straight from the barbecue, leftover roasted beef sandwiches or a fragrant stir-fry, beef is such a flavour-packed ingredient.

ABOVE
Tying a roast will hold the shape while the meat becomes juicy and tender. You can also tie herbs or bacon around the beef for extra flavour.

LEFT
When you brown meat, you are actually caramelising the outside to form a crust. This process gives the meat plenty of flavour.

lamb

fast flat-roasted lamb

With salty feta, olives and tangy sumac, this simple barbecued salad isn't short on flavour.

grilled lamb with olive and rocket salad

fast flat-roasted lamb

2 teaspoons ground cumin
1 teaspoon smoked paprika*
1 tablespoon brown sugar
1 teaspoon cracked black pepper
½ teaspoon sea salt flakes
16 sprigs oregano
1kg boned lamb leg, butterflied and trimmed
store-bought baba ghanoush*, flat bread* and lemon wedges, to serve

Preheat oven to 220°C (425°F). Combine the cumin, paprika, sugar, pepper and salt and rub over both sides of the lamb. Place the oregano in an oiled baking dish and top with the lamb. Roast for 20 minutes for medium or until cooked to your liking. Rest the lamb, covered, for 5 minutes before slicing. Divide the lamb between plates and serve with the baba ghanoush, flat bread, lemon wedges and a tomato and mint salad, if desired. SERVES 4.

grilled lamb with olive and rocket salad

600g lamb backstrap (boneless loin)
1 tablespoon olive oil
2 tablespoons lemon juice
1 tablespoon honey
1 tablespoon za'atar*, plus extra, for sprinkling
lemon wedges, to serve
olive and rocket salad
100g rocket (arugula) leaves
250g cherry tomatoes, quartered
200g firm feta
½ cup (60g) pitted olives, chopped
2 tablespoons olive oil
1 tablespoon red wine vinegar

Place the lamb in a bowl with the oil, lemon juice and honey and toss to coat. Sprinkle with za'atar and cook on a preheated char-grill pan or barbecue over high heat for 3–4 minutes each side for medium or until cooked to your liking. Divide the rocket, tomatoes, feta and olives between plates and drizzle with the combined olive oil and vinegar. Slice the lamb and serve with the salad, extra za'atar and lemon wedges. SERVES 4.

lamb racks with warm parsnip salad

2 x 400g (6 cutlet) lamb racks, trimmed
⅓ cup (80ml) red wine vinegar
⅓ cup finely chopped mint leaves
1 tablespoon seeded mustard
2 tablespoons caster (superfine) sugar
4 parsnips, peeled and quartered
4 green onions (scallions), trimmed and halved
2 tablespoons vegetable oil
8 sprigs marjoram or oregano
sea salt and cracked black pepper

Preheat oven to 200°C (400°F). Using a small, sharp knife, score the fat of the lamb racks. Combine the vinegar, mint, mustard and sugar and place in a shallow ceramic dish. Add the lamb racks, fat-side down, and marinate for 15 minutes.

Place the parsnips and onions in a bowl with the oil, marjoram, salt and pepper and toss to combine. Place on a baking tray lined with non-stick baking paper.

Remove the lamb from the marinade, reserving the marinade, and place on a separate baking tray. Place the lamb and parsnips in the oven and bake for 30 minutes or until the parsnips are golden and the lamb is cooked to your liking.

While the lamb is cooking, place the reserved marinade in a saucepan and bring to the boil over high heat. Cook for 2 minutes or until reduced slightly. Slice the lamb into cutlets and divide between plates with the parsnips and green onions. Spoon over the sauce to serve. SERVES 4.

Classic minted lamb roast gets a speedy makeover with these quick roasting racks teamed with sweet parsnips and green onions.

lamb racks with warm parsnip salad

lemon rice salad with minted lamb

5 cups cooked rice (330g uncooked rice)
250g snow peas (mange tout), blanched and shredded
2 tablespoons lemon juice
2 teaspoons finely grated lemon rind
1 tablespoon honey
1 tablespoon olive oil
sea salt and cracked black pepper
minted lamb
500g lamb backstrap (boneless loin)
1 tablespoon Dijon mustard
1 tablespoon honey, extra
½ cup shredded mint leaves

To make the rice salad, combine the rice, snow peas, lemon juice, rind, honey, oil, salt and pepper and toss to combine. Set aside.

To make the minted lamb, heat a non-stick frying pan over high heat. Sprinkle the lamb with salt and pepper. Cook the lamb for 3–4 minutes each side for medium or until cooked to your liking. Rest the lamb for 5 minutes before slicing. Combine the mustard, extra honey and mint and toss with the lamb. Divide the rice salad between plates and top with the minted lamb to serve. SERVES 4.

lamb with couscous and spiced almonds

150g blanched almonds
2 teaspoons sesame seeds
1 teaspoon ground cumin
1 tablespoon olive oil
2 tablespoons honey
2 x 250g lamb backstraps (boneless loin)
extra olive oil, for brushing
sea salt and cracked black pepper
4 cups cooked instant couscous (400g uncooked couscous)
1 cup mint leaves
store-bought tzatziki*, to serve

Preheat oven to 180°C (350°F). Place the almonds, sesame seeds, cumin, oil and honey in a bowl and toss to coat. Place the mixture on a baking tray lined with non-stick baking paper and bake for 10 minutes or until golden. Cool, roughly chop and set aside.

Brush the lamb with a little oil and sprinkle with salt and pepper. Cook on a preheated char-grill pan or barbecue over high heat for 3–4 minutes each side for medium or until cooked to your liking. Cover and rest for 4 minutes before slicing. Divide the couscous between plates and top with the mint and sliced lamb. Sprinkle with the spicy almond mixture and serve with tzatziki. SERVES 4.

lamb cutlets with sticky balsamic figs

2 x 400g (6 cutlet) lamb racks, trimmed
olive oil, for brushing
2 teaspoons chopped rosemary leaves
sea salt and cracked black pepper
sticky balsamic figs
¾ cup (180ml) balsamic vinegar
2 tablespoons brown sugar
2 teaspoons rosemary leaves, extra
1 tablespoon seeded mustard
4 fresh figs, halved

Preheat oven to 180°C (350°F). Brush the lamb with oil and sprinkle with rosemary, salt and pepper. Heat a non-stick frying pan over high heat. Add the lamb racks, one at a time, and cook for 2–3 minutes each side or until browned. Place in a baking dish in the oven and roast for 10 minutes for medium or until cooked to your liking.

Wipe out the frying pan with absorbent paper and add the vinegar, sugar, extra rosemary and mustard. Simmer over high heat for 2–3 minutes or until the mixture is syrupy. Add the figs, cut-side down, and cook for 2–3 minutes each side or until golden and sticky. Cut the lamb into cutlets, divide between plates and spoon over the figs. Serve with crispy parsnip chips, if desired. SERVES 4.

pine nut and honey crumbed lamb cutlets

60g butter
1 tablespoon honey
⅓ cup (50g) pine nuts
1 tablespoon thyme leaves
sea salt and cracked black pepper
2 cups (140g) fresh breadcrumbs
8–12 x 75g lamb cutlets, trimmed
lemon wedges, to serve

Preheat oven to 200°C (400°F). Melt the butter and honey in a saucepan over low heat. Add the pine nuts, thyme, salt and pepper and stir to combine. Place the breadcrumbs in a bowl, add the butter mixture and toss to combine.

Place the lamb on a baking tray lined with non-stick baking paper and top with the breadcrumb mixture. Roast for 12–15 minutes or until the lamb is cooked to your liking and the crumbs are golden. Serve with lemon wedges and a simple tomato, basil and red onion salad, if desired. SERVES 4.

maple mustard lamb skewers

lamb, eggplant and feta bake

maple mustard lamb skewers

1kg boneless lamb shoulder, trimmed and thinly sliced
⅓ cup (80ml) maple syrup
2 tablespoons Dijon mustard
2 tablespoons white wine vinegar
1 tablespoon rosemary leaves
store-bought baba ghanoush*, sliced feta, finely sliced celery
  and olives, to serve

Place the lamb, maple syrup, mustard, vinegar and rosemary in
a bowl, toss to coat and marinate for 20 minutes. Preheat a grill
(broiler) on high heat. Thread the lamb onto skewers and place on
a wire rack on a baking tray and grill (broil) for 6 minutes or until
cooked to your liking. Serve the lamb skewers with baba ghanoush,
feta, finely sliced celery and olives. SERVES 4.

lamb, eggplant and feta bake

1 tablespoon olive oil
1 brown onion, chopped
1 tablespoon oregano leaves
2 cloves garlic, crushed
750g lamb mince (ground lamb)
1 cup (250ml) chicken stock
2 tablespoons balsamic vinegar
500g cherry tomatoes, halved
1 eggplant (aubergine), chopped
175g firm feta, chopped
¼ cup (60ml) olive oil, extra
2 tablespoons rosemary leaves
sea salt and cracked black pepper

Preheat oven to 220°C (425°F). Heat the oil in a non-stick frying
pan over medium heat. Add the onion and oregano and cook for
7 minutes or until golden. Increase heat to high, add the garlic and
lamb and cook for 8–10 minutes or until well browned. Add the
stock, vinegar and tomatoes and cook for 5–6 minutes or until
the lamb is tender.

Divide the lamb mixture between 4 x 1½-cup (375ml) capacity
ovenproof dishes or 1 x 1.5-litre capacity dish. Place the eggplant,
feta, extra oil, rosemary, salt and pepper in a bowl and toss to coat.
Top the lamb with the eggplant mixture and bake for 25 minutes
or until the topping is golden. SERVES 4.

lamb and feta burgers

500g lamb mince (ground lamb)
1½ tablespoons redcurrant jelly
½ cup (35g) fresh breadcrumbs
2 tablespoons oregano leaves, chopped
1 egg
100g feta, crumbled
sea salt and cracked black pepper
olive oil, for brushing
2 large green tomatoes, thickly sliced
4 burger buns, halved
⅓ cup (100g) store-bought aïoli
rocket (arugula) leaves, to serve

Place the lamb, redcurrant jelly, breadcrumbs, oregano, egg, feta,
salt and pepper in a bowl and mix to combine. Shape into 4 equal-
sized patties and brush with a little oil. Heat a non-stick frying pan
over medium heat. Add the patties and cook for 5 minutes each
side or until cooked through. Set aside and keep warm.

Wipe out the pan with absorbent paper and increase heat to high.
Brush the tomatoes with oil and cook for 1–2 minutes each side
or until golden. To assemble, spread one half of the buns with aïoli
and top with the rocket, patties, tomatoes and remaining bun halves
to serve. SERVES 4.

spiced lamb pies

12 sheets store-bought filo pastry*, thawed
melted butter, for brushing
400g lamb mince (ground lamb)
1 cup (70g) fresh breadcrumbs
1 tablespoon harissa*
1 tablespoon honey
¼ cup (40g) pine nuts
¼ cup chopped mint leaves
¼ cup chopped dill
sea salt and cracked black pepper
150g feta, roughly chopped
lemon wedges, to serve

Preheat oven to 200°C (400°F). Brush a sheet of filo pastry with
butter and top with another sheet of pastry. Repeat until you have
a stack of 6 sheets. Repeat with remaining pastry to make another
stack and cut both stacks in half so you have 4 rectangles. Place the
pastry into 4 x 1½-cup (375ml) capacity pie dishes.

Place the lamb, breadcrumbs, harissa, honey, pine nuts, mint, dill,
salt and pepper in a bowl and mix well to combine. Stir though the
feta. Divide the lamb between the pie dishes. Fold over the pastry to
enclose the filling. Place the pies on a baking tray and brush the tops
with butter. Score the tops of the pies and bake for 20 minutes or
until pastry is golden. SERVES 4.

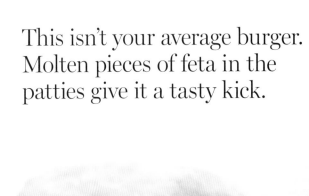

This isn't your average burger. Molten pieces of feta in the patties give it a tasty kick.

lamb and feta burgers

spiced lamb pies

tips & tricks

RIGHT
Lamb works really well with tangy flavours of lemon and vinegar, as well as mint, mustard and even sweet honey.

BELOW
For a traditional leg of lamb, roast it on rosemary sprigs to act as a roasting rack. Allow 18–20 minutes per 500g of meat for medium cooked.

There's nothing quite like the Sunday lamb roast with all the trimmings. This sweet, tender and succulent meat is a family favourite.

ABOVE
Lamb cutlets, racks, chops and leg steaks are all perfect for the barbecue, while shoulders and legs are great for slow roasting.

LEFT
For succulent and juicy roasted lamb, it is best cooked to medium and allowed to rest, covered, for 10–20 minutes so the juices can settle.

pork

The sweet potato gives this pork curry a sweet mellow flavour to balance the heat from the chilli.

pork and sweet potato curry

asian pork spare ribs

pork and sweet potato curry

¼ cup store-bought Thai red curry paste
1 kg pork neck or shoulder, trimmed and cut into cubes
1 tablespoon finely grated ginger
8 kaffir lime leaves*, lightly crushed
2 cups (500ml) coconut cream
2 cups (500ml) chicken stock
700g sweet potato (kumara), peeled and sliced
2 tablespoons lime juice
1 tablespoon fish sauce
1 tablespoon brown sugar
½ cup coriander (cilantro) leaves
½ cup Thai basil leaves
½ cup mint leaves
2 green onions (scallions), trimmed and shredded
steamed jasmine rice, to serve

Heat a large deep non-stick frying pan or wok over medium–high heat. Add the curry paste and cook for 1 minute or until fragrant. Add the pork and cook, stirring, for 4 minutes or until the pork is well coated. Add the ginger, lime leaf, coconut cream and stock and simmer, covered, for 20 minutes. Add the sweet potato, cover, and simmer for a further 15 minutes or until the pork and potato are tender. Stir through the lime juice, fish sauce and brown sugar. Spoon the curry into bowls and top with coriander, basil, mint and onion and serve with steamed jasmine rice. SERVES 4.

asian pork spare ribs

12 x 120g Chinese pork spare ribs
4 star anise
12 slices ginger
marinade
1 cup (250ml) kecap manis*
¼ cup (60ml) honey
2 tablespoons finely grated ginger
3 teaspoons dried chilli flakes
2 teaspoons Chinese five-spice powder*
steamed Asian greens, to serve

Place the ribs in a large deep saucepan and add enough water to cover. Add the star anise and ginger, cover, and bring to the boil. Reduce heat and simmer for 45 minutes. Drain and set aside. Preheat oven to 180°C (350°F). Place the ribs on a baking tray lined with non-stick baking paper. To make the marinade, combine the kecap manis, honey, ginger, chilli and five-spice and brush generously over both sides of the ribs. Roast for 15 minutes each side or until the ribs are sticky and golden. Serve with steamed Asian greens. SERVES 4.

caramelised chilli pork neck

1 tablespoon vegetable oil
1kg pork neck, trimmed and cut into large pieces
3 cloves garlic, sliced
5 long red chillies*, seeds removed and sliced
4 large pieces orange rind
2 tablespoons shredded ginger
1½ cups (375ml) Chinese cooking wine* (Shaoxing)
¼ cup (60ml) soy sauce
1¼ cups (310ml) chicken stock
¼ cup (60g) grated palm sugar* or brown sugar
steamed jasmine rice and Asian greens, to serve

Heat the oil in a large deep non-stick frying pan over high heat. Add the pork and cook for 5–7 minutes or until well browned, remove from the pan and set aside. Wipe out the pan with absorbent paper and add the garlic, chilli, orange rind, ginger, wine, soy, stock and sugar and bring to a simmer. Return the pork to the pan, reduce heat, cover, and simmer for 50 minutes or until the pork is tender. Serve the pork with the pan sauce, steamed jasmine rice and Asian greens. SERVES 4.

This tender caramelised pork should come with a warning. It's seriously addictive.

caramelised chilli pork neck

pork pasties

2 teaspoons fennel seeds
400g pork mince (ground pork)
1 cup (70g) fresh breadcrumbs
1 tablespoon honey
1 tablespoon chopped sage leaves
sea salt and cracked black pepper
4 x sheets store-bought shortcrust pastry, thawed
1 egg, lightly beaten

Preheat oven to 180°C (350°F). Place the fennel seeds in a mortar
and pestle and crush lightly. Place the fennel, pork, breadcrumbs,
honey, sage, salt and pepper in a bowl and mix well to combine.
   Cut 4 x 20cm circles from the pastry. Place a quarter of the pork
mixture on one half of each of the circles. Brush the edges with the
egg, fold over and press to seal, pressing the edges with a fork. Place
on baking trays lined with non-stick baking paper and brush with
the egg. Bake for 30 minutes or until the pastry is golden. Serve
the pasties with a rocket and apple salad, if desired. SERVES 4

maple-glazed pork and pancetta meatloaf

24 slices flat pancetta*
1½ cups (105g) fresh breadcrumbs
¼ cup (60ml) milk
500g pork mince (ground pork)
375g veal mince (ground veal)
2 tablespoons Dijon mustard
1 egg
1 tablespoon thyme leaves
sea salt and cracked black pepper
2 tablespoons maple syrup
mashed potato, to serve

Preheat oven to 160°C (325°F). Line a 22cm x 8cm loaf tin with the
pancetta. Place the breadcrumbs in a bowl, pour over the milk and
stand until milk has absorbed. Add the pork and veal mince, mustard,
egg, thyme, salt and pepper and mix well to combine. Press into
the tin and fold over any overhanging ends of pancetta. Bake for 30
minutes or until the meat is just cooked through. Invert the meatloaf
onto a baking tray and brush with the maple syrup. Increase the heat
to 180°C (350°F) and bake for 15–20 minutes or until the pancetta
is golden. Slice and serve with mashed potato. SERVES 4.

chilli jam pork with rice noodle rolls

1 tablespoon vegetable oil
⅓ cup (110g) chilli jam*
2 tablespoons shredded ginger
500g pork mince (ground pork)
1 cup (200g) sliced water chestnuts*
½ cup (125ml) chicken stock
1kg fresh rice noodle rolls*
sliced green onions (scallions) and coriander (cilantro) leaves,
  to serve

Heat the oil in a large non-stick frying pan over high heat. Add the
chilli jam and ginger and cook for 2 minutes. Add the pork and cook,
stirring, for 5 minutes or until cooked through. Add the chestnuts
and stock and cook for 5 minutes.
    Cook the rice noodles according to packet instructions. Divide
the noodles between plates and top with the pork, green onion
and coriander. Serve with steamed broccolini, if desired. SERVES 4.

crispy pork wontons

300g pork mince (ground pork)
2 tablespoons chilli jam*
2 green onions (scallions), trimmed and chopped
1 tablespoon grated ginger
40 store-bought wonton wrappers*
vegetable oil, for brushing
600g gai larn*, trimmed
1 long red chilli*, sliced
2 green onions (scallions), extra, trimmed and sliced
2 tablespoons soy sauce
2 teaspoons sesame oil
hoisin sauce, to serve

Preheat oven to 160°C (325°F). Place the pork, chilli jam, onion and
ginger in a bowl and mix well to combine. Place 1 tablespoon of the
mixture in the centre of half the wrappers. Top with the remaining
wrappers and press to seal. Place the wontons on baking trays lined
with non-stick baking paper and brush both sides with a little oil.
Bake for 25 minutes or until golden and cooked through. Blanch
the gai larn and divide between plates. Sprinkle with chilli and extra
onion and drizzle with soy and sesame oil. Serve the wontons with the
gai larn and hoisin sauce, for dipping. SERVES 4.

vietnamese pork skewers

gourmet pork burgers

vietnamese pork skewers

1kg pork shoulder, trimmed and thinly sliced
3 green onions (scallions), trimmed and finely chopped
1 stalk lemongrass, trimmed and finely chopped
2 cloves garlic, crushed
⅓ cup (80ml) fish sauce*
⅓ cup (55g) brown sugar
baguette slices, to serve
pickled carrot
½ cup (125ml) white vinegar
2 tablespoons white sugar
4 carrots, peeled and shredded with a mandolin
1 cup coriander (cilantro) leaves
2 long red chillies*, sliced

Combine the pork, onion, lemongrass, garlic, fish sauce and brown sugar in a bowl and refrigerate for 20 minutes to marinate.

To make the pickled carrot, place the vinegar and white sugar in a saucepan over medium heat and bring to a rapid simmer. Simmer until the sugar dissolves and refrigerate until chilled. Toss the cooled syrup with the carrot, coriander and chilli.

Thread the pork onto skewers and cook on a preheated char-grill pan or barbecue over high heat for 2 minutes each side or until just cooked through. Serve the pork with the baguette and the pickled carrot. SERVES 4.

gourmet pork burgers

1 cup (70g) fresh breadcrumbs
2 tablespoons milk
450g pork mince (ground pork)
1 tablespoon quince paste*
1 teaspoon chopped rosemary leaves
sea salt and cracked black pepper
4 bread rolls, halved and toasted
⅓ cup (90g) store-bought caramelised onion relish*
8 radicchio leaves
4 large slices blue cheese*

Place the breadcrumbs in a bowl, sprinkle over the milk and stand for 5 minutes until milk has absorbed. Add the pork, quince paste, rosemary, salt and pepper and mix well to combine. Divide the mixture into 4 and shape into patties. Heat a non-stick frying pan, barbecue or char-grill pan over medium–high heat. Cook the patties for 4 minutes each side or until just cooked through. Divide the rolls between plates, spread the bases with relish and top with the radicchio. Top with the patties, blue cheese and remaining bread. Serve with potato chips, if desired. SERVES 4.

roasted apple and quince pork cutlets

4 x 280g pork cutlets, skin on
olive oil, for brushing
sea salt and cracked black pepper
100g quince paste*
12 thin slices apple
1 tablespoon oregano leaves
50g butter, melted

Preheat oven to 220°C (425°F). Using a small, sharp knife, score the fat and rind of the cutlets. Brush the rind with oil and place on a baking tray lined with non-stick baking paper. Sprinkle with salt and pepper and spread the flesh with a little quince paste. Top with apple slices and oregano and brush with butter. Roast for 20 minutes or until the skin is crisp and the apple is golden. Serve with steamed greens, if desired. SERVES 4.

chinese pork in paper

2 x 400g pork fillet (tenderloin), trimmed and halved
¼ cup (60ml) char sui (Chinese barbecue sauce)
2 tablespoons oyster sauce
¼ cup shredded ginger
4 green onions (scallions), trimmed and sliced
4 star anise
4 cinnamon sticks
600g choy sum or gai larn*, halved
2 tablespoons shredded ginger, extra
⅓ cup (60ml) oyster sauce
1 tablespoon Chinese cooking wine* (Shaoxing)
1 teaspoon sesame oil

Preheat oven to 160°C (325°F). Cut 4 large sheets of non-stick baking paper and place a piece of pork on each sheet of paper. Combine the char sui and oyster sauce and spoon over the pork. Top each fillet with ginger, onion, a star anise and a cinnamon stick. Fold over the paper to enclose the pork and form a parcel to seal. Place on a baking tray and bake for 10 minutes.

While the pork is cooking, cut 4 more sheets of paper and divide the greens between the paper. Top with the extra ginger, oyster sauce, cooking wine and sesame oil and form a parcel to seal. Place on the tray with the pork and cook for a further 15 minutes or until the pork and greens are tender. Divide the parcels between plates and serve with steamed rice, if desired. SERVES 4.

roasted apple and quince pork cutlets

The beauty of these chic parcels
is that the main and side dishes
are cooked at the same time.

chinese pork in paper

tips & tricks

RIGHT
Pork is the perfect partner for sweet and robust flavours, such as apple or quince paste, and matches well with a fragrant sage stuffing.

BELOW
If you don't have time to roast a whole loin but still want to enjoy crackling, choose pork chops or cutlets with the skin on. Score, oil and roast the chops for the same effect.

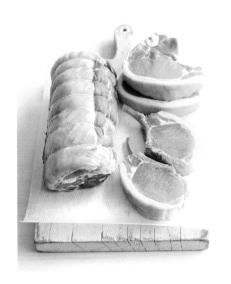

A piece of roasted pork with crackling and apple sauce is one of life's true pleasures. One of the most versatile meats, pork is a cook's best friend.

ABOVE
When pork is fully cooked, it should still have a pink blush, which shows that it's juicy and succulent.

LEFT
For the best crackling, place salted pork skin in the fridge overnight to dry it out. This ensures the crispiest surface. Scoring also helps to give it crunch.

fish & seafood

sesame-crusted salmon with preserved lemon and zucchini salad

This is the new Aussie prawn on the barbecue, fragrant with fresh and robust Asian flavours.

lime and lemongrass prawns

sesame-crusted salmon with preserved lemon and zucchini salad

4 x 200g salmon fillets, skin on
1 tablespoon wasabi*
½ cup (75g) sesame seeds
vegetable oil, for brushing
preserved lemon and zucchini salad
3 zucchinis (courgettes), thinly sliced lengthways
  with a vegetable peeler
2 tablespoons shredded preserved lemon rind*
½ cup shredded mint leaves
1 tablespoon olive oil
2 teaspoons lemon juice
sea salt and cracked black pepper

To make the preserved lemon and zucchini salad, place the zucchini, preserved lemon and mint in a bowl. Combine the oil, lemon juice, salt and pepper, pour over the salad and toss to combine.

Heat a non-stick frying pan over medium–high heat. Spread the flesh side of the salmon with wasabi and press into the sesame seeds. Brush both sides of the salmon with a little oil, add to the pan, skin-side down, and cook for 4–5 minutes or until the skin is crisp. Turn salmon and cook for a further 1–2 minutes or until the sesame is golden and salmon is cooked to your liking. Serve the salmon with the preserved lemon and zucchini salad. SERVES 4.

lime and lemongrass prawns

2 stalks lemongrass*, trimmed and chopped
4 kaffir lime leaves*, sliced
2 long green chillies*, chopped
sea salt
2 tablespoons vegetable oil
24 green (raw) prawns (shrimp), peeled, with tails intact
¼ cup (60ml) coconut cream
1 long green chilli*, extra, seeds removed and chopped
2½ cups cooked jasmine rice (150g uncooked rice)
lime wedges, to serve

Place the lemongrass, lime leaf, chilli, salt and oil in a small food processor and process until finely chopped. Thread the prawns onto skewers and spread with the lemongrass mixture. Heat a grill (broiler), char-grill pan or barbecue over high heat and cook the prawns for 1–2 minutes each side or until just cooked through.

Stir the coconut cream, extra chilli and a little salt through the cooked rice. Divide the rice and prawn skewers between plates and serve with lime wedges and a cucumber and mint salad, if desired. SERVES 4.

crispy fish sliders

8 x 125g small white fish fillets, skin off
¼ cup (50g) rice flour, for dusting
½ cup (100g) rice flour, extra
¾ cup (180ml) cold sparkling mineral water
sea salt and cracked black pepper
vegetable oil, for shallow frying
8 small soft bread rolls, halved
8 butter lettuce leaves
tartare sauce
½ cup (150g) whole-egg mayonnaise
6 cornichons, chopped
1 tablespoon salted capers, rinsed and chopped
1 tablespoon chopped dill
1 tablespoon lemon juice

To make the tartare sauce, place the mayonnaise, cornichons, capers, dill and lemon in a bowl and mix to combine. Set aside.

Dust the fish in the rice flour, shaking off any excess. Place the extra rice flour in a bowl, add the mineral water, season with salt and pepper and whisk until smooth.

Heat 2cm of oil in a deep frying pan over high heat. Dip the fish in the batter and cook in the hot oil, in batches, for 2 minutes each side or until crisp and golden. Drain on absorbent paper. Spread the bread rolls with the tartare sauce and top with the lettuce and fish. Serve with thin potato chips, if desired. SERVES 4.

It's official – these hand-sized crispy fish sliders with tangy tartare sauce are my new summer burger of choice.

crispy fish sliders

miso-grilled fish

4 x 200g firm white fish fillets, skin off
¼ cup white miso paste*
2 tablespoons caster (superfine) sugar
1 tablespoon finely grated ginger
1 tablespoon vegetable oil
2 tablespoons water
steamed jasmine rice and lemon wedges, to serve

Place the fish on a baking tray lined with non-stick baking paper. Combine the miso, sugar, ginger, oil and water and spread over the fish. Allow to marinate for 10–15 minutes. Preheat a grill (broiler) over high heat and grill (broil) the fish for 6–8 minutes or until fish is just cooked through. Serve the fish with steamed rice and lemon wedges and a simple cucumber salad with a toasted sesame seed dressing, if desired. SERVES 4.

salmon and dill pie

½ cup chopped dill leaves
1 cup (240g) sour cream
2 tablespoons Dijon mustard
2 tablespoons store-bought grated horseradish*
¼ cup (50g) salted capers, rinsed and chopped
2 tablespoons finely grated lemon rind
sea salt and cracked black pepper
2 sheets store-bought puff pastry, thawed
4 x 200g salmon fillets, skin off
1 egg, lightly beaten, for brushing

Preheat oven to 180°C (350°F). Combine the dill, sour cream, mustard, horseradish, capers, lemon rind, salt and pepper and set aside. Cut each pastry sheet into quarters. Place a tablespoonful of the dill mixture on 4 pieces of the pastry. Top with a piece of salmon and the remaining dill mixture. Top with remaining pastry and press edges to seal. Place on baking trays lined with non-stick baking paper and brush with the egg. Bake for 20 minutes or until pastry is puffed and golden. Serve the pies with a simple green salad, if desired. SERVES 4.

smoked trout and fennel niçoise salad

1 cup flat-leaf parsley leaves
½ cup (90g) finely sliced cornichons
12 baby (new) potatoes, cooked and thickly sliced
2 tablespoons salted capers, rinsed
2 bulbs baby fennel
4 hot smoked river trout fillets, roughly flaked
2 soft boiled eggs, peeled and halved
lemon and dill dressing
¼ cup (60ml) olive oil
2 tablespoons lemon juice
2 tablespoons finely chopped dill leaves
2 teaspoons Dijon mustard
sea salt and cracked black pepper

To make the lemon and dill dressing, whisk together the oil, lemon juice, dill, mustard, salt and pepper and set aside.

Place the parsley, cornichons, potatoes and capers in a bowl. Using a mandolin, finely slice the fennel, add to the potato mixture and toss to combine. Divide the potato salad between plates, top with the trout and egg and spoon over the dressing. Serve with crusty bread, if desired. SERVES 4.

mussels in chilli coconut broth

2 teaspoons vegetable oil
2 long red chillies*, shredded
4 kaffir lime leaves*, shredded
1 tablespoon shredded ginger
1 cup (250ml) coconut milk
1 tablespoon fish sauce
2 tablespoons lime juice
1kg mussels, cleaned
coriander (cilantro) leaves, Thai basil leaves and
   lime wedges, to serve

Heat the oil in a large, deep frying pan or wok over medium–high heat. Add the chilli, lime leaf and ginger and cook for 1–2 minutes. Add the coconut milk, fish sauce and lime juice and bring to a simmer. Add the mussels, cover and cook for 3–5 minutes or until the mussels open. Spoon into bowls and serve with coriander, basil and lime wedges. SERVES 4.

With its sticky-sweet sauce, crispy
texture and spicy chilli heat, this
is my favourite way to eat fish.

crispy fish with sweet chilli vinegar glaze

thai-style baked fish

crispy fish with sweet chilli vinegar glaze

¼ cup (50g) rice flour
sea salt and cracked black pepper
12 x 120g whiting fillets
vegetable oil, for shallow frying
¾ cup coriander (cilantro) leaves
4 green onions (scallions), trimmed and sliced
steamed jasmine rice, to serve
sweet chilli vinegar glaze
4 long red chillies*, seeds removed and sliced
¼ cup shredded ginger
4 kaffir lime leaves*, shredded
1 cup (250ml) white wine vinegar
½ cup (110g) white sugar

To make the sweet chilli vinegar glaze, place the chilli, ginger, lime leaf, vinegar and sugar in a saucepan over medium heat and bring to the boil. Rapidly simmer for 20 minutes or until thickened. Remove from the heat and set aside.

Combine the rice flour, salt and pepper. Dust the fish with the flour, shaking off any excess. Heat 1cm of oil in a large frying pan over high heat. Add the fish and cook, in batches, for 2 minutes each side or until crisp. Divide the fish between plates, spoon over the glaze and top with coriander and green onion. Serve with rice. SERVES 4.

thai-style baked fish

6 stalks lemongrass*, halved lengthways
12 kaffir lime leaves*
1 large (1kg) fillet firm white fish, skin on
¼ cup store-bought Thai red curry paste
2 tablespoons shredded ginger
3 cloves garlic, sliced
2 long red chillies*, seeds removed and chopped
2 tablespoons vegetable oil
1 cup coriander (cilantro) leaves
1 cup mint leaves
1 cup Thai basil leaves
steamed jasmine rice and lime wedges, to serve

Preheat oven to 200°C (400°F). Place the lemongrass and lime leaf on a baking tray lined with non-stick baking paper and top with the fish, skin-side down. Spread the flesh of the fish with the curry paste. Combine the ginger, garlic, chilli and oil. Sprinkle over the fish and bake for 20–30 minutes or until the fish is just cooked through. Top the fish with the coriander, mint and Thai basil and serve with steamed rice and lime wedges. SERVES 4.

grilled lemon snapper with potato and horseradish salad

3 tablespoons olive oil
1½ tablespoons grated lemon rind
sea salt and cracked black pepper
8 x 100g snapper fillets, skin on
potato and horseradish salad
½ cup (150g) whole-egg mayonnaise
1 tablespoon store-bought grated horseradish*
2 tablespoons lemon juice
12 baby (new) potatoes, cooked and halved
⅓ cup flat-leaf parsley leaves

Combine the oil, lemon rind, salt and pepper and brush over the fish. Heat a non-stick frying pan over high heat and cook the fish, skin-side down, for 3 minutes each side or until cooked to your liking.

While the fish is cooking, make the potato and horseradish salad. Combine the mayonnaise, horseradish and lemon juice, pour over the potatoes and toss with the parsley, salt and pepper to combine. Serve the fish with the salad. SERVES 4.

tuna and edamame salad with chilli ponzu dressing

300g frozen edamame*
8 red radishes, thinly sliced
100g mizuna leaves*
1 x 400g piece sashimi-grade tuna
¼ cup (35g) sesame seeds
2 teaspoons vegetable oil
chilli ponzu dressing
2 teaspoons dried chilli flakes
2 tablespoons lemon juice
1 tablespoon soy sauce
¼ cup (60ml) mirin*

Place the edamame in a bowl, cover with boiling salted water and allow to stand for 5 minutes or until tender. Drain and rinse under cold water to refresh. Toss the edamame with the radish and mizuna and divide between plates.

Roll the tuna in the sesame seeds to coat. Heat the oil in a large non-stick frying pan over high heat, add the tuna and cook for 1–2 minutes each side or until well seared. Rest for 5 minutes before thinly slicing.

To make the chilli ponzu dressing, combine the chilli flakes, lemon, soy and mirin. Top the salad with the tuna slices and spoon over the dressing to serve. SERVES 4.

The horseradish is the secret kick in this potato salad and it goes perfectly with the fish.

grilled lemon snapper with potato and horseradish salad

tuna and edamame salad with chilli ponzu dressing

tips & tricks

RIGHT
To remove any small bones in a fish fillet, run your hand down the length of the fish and remove any protruding bones with kitchen tweezers.

BELOW
To ensure crispy skin when you cook fish, rub the skin with oil and sprinkle with sea salt. Cook on high heat, skin-side down, until crisp, then turn.

I love that seafood lends itself to fast and fresh meals, whether it's simple sashimi, a prawn pasta or a whole-baked fish.

ABOVE
Fresh fish should have bright, clear eyes, not glazed. The flesh should be nice and shiny and it should smell of the sea.

LEFT
When choosing prawns, they should be firm and have no discolouration around the legs or head.

vegetables

With a burst of lemon and creamy goat's curd, this chic salad is simple yet full of flavour.

swiss chard salad with goat's cheese croutons

roasted asparagus, ricotta and prosciutto toasts

swiss chard salad with goat's cheese croutons

16 slices baguette
120g soft goat's cheese*
200g small rainbow Swiss chard*, trimmed
150g green beans, trimmed
150g yellow beans, trimmed
¼ cup (60ml) olive oil
1 tablespoon finely grated lemon rind
1 tablespoon white balsamic vinegar
sea salt and cracked black pepper

Spread the baguette slices with the goat's cheese and place under a preheated hot grill (broiler) and cook for 2 minutes or until golden. Set aside.

Blanch the chard and beans in boiling water until just tender, drain and refresh in cold water. Divide the chard and beans between plates. Whisk to combine the oil, lemon rind, vinegar, salt and pepper and spoon over the vegetables. Top with the goat's cheese croutons to serve. SERVES 4.

roasted asparagus, ricotta and prosciutto toasts

1 cup (200g) fresh ricotta
1 egg, lightly beaten
2 teaspoons finely grated lemon rind
2 tablespoons finely chopped flat-leaf parsley leaves
24 spears asparagus, trimmed
8 slices prosciutto
4 very large slices crusty bread
⅓ cup (80ml) good-quality store-bought basil pesto
olive oil, for drizzling

Preheat oven to 200°C (400°F). Combine the ricotta, egg, lemon rind and parsley. Place 3 spears of asparagus on each slice of prosciutto and top with a large spoonful of the ricotta mixture. Wrap the prosciutto over to enclose the filling.

Spread each bread slice with pesto and place in a baking dish. Top with the prosciutto and asparagus parcels, drizzle with oil and roast for 30 minutes or until the asparagus is tender and the prosciutto is crisp. Serve with a rocket (arugula) salad, if desired. SERVES 4.

free-form ratatouille tart

2 sheets store-bought shortcrust pastry, thawed
2 cups (400g) fresh ricotta
½ cup shredded basil leaves
½ cup (40g) finely grated pecorino*
2 baby eggplant (aubergine), thinly sliced
2 zucchinis (courgettes), thinly sliced
8 cherry tomatoes, sliced
⅓ cup oregano leaves
olive oil, for sprinkling
sea salt and cracked black pepper

Preheat oven to 180°C (350°F). Cut the pastry into 2 x 26cm rounds and place on baking trays lined with non-stick baking paper. Combine the ricotta, basil and pecorino and spread over the base of each pastry round, leaving a 5cm border.

Place the eggplant slices, overlapping, in a round starting from the outside of the ricotta. Then make overlapping rounds of the zucchini and the tomato. Sprinkle the vegetables with oregano, oil, salt and pepper. Fold over the pastry border and pinch the edges to form a crust. Bake for 30 minutes or until the pastry is golden and the vegetables are soft. Cut into quarters to serve. SERVES 4.

The classic ratatouille gets a fresh makeover with this simple spring tart on a light ricotta base.

free-form ratatouille tart

gorgonzola polenta with garlic roasted mushrooms

8 small flat mushrooms
12 Swiss brown mushrooms
12 button mushrooms
40g butter, melted
1 tablespoon olive oil
4 cloves garlic, thinly sliced
½ cup sage leaves
gorgonzola polenta
2 cups (500ml) milk
2 cups (500ml) chicken stock
1 cup (170g) instant polenta
sea salt and cracked black pepper
4 thin slices gorgonzola*, to serve

Preheat oven to 200°C (400°F). Place the mushrooms, butter, oil, garlic and sage on a baking tray lined with non-stick baking paper and toss to coat. Bake for 20 minutes or until golden. To make the polenta, place the milk and stock in a saucepan over medium–high heat and bring to the boil. Whisk in the polenta and stir for 3 minutes or until creamy. Sprinkle with salt and pepper. Divide between plates, top with the gorgonzola and roasted mushrooms to serve. SERVES 4.

three pea salad with feta pastries

1 sheet store-bought puff pastry, thawed and cut into 4
200g feta, sliced
150g snow peas (mange tout), trimmed and blanched
200g sugar snap peas, trimmed and blanched
1½ cups (180g) frozen peas, thawed
snow pea shoots, to serve
mint salsa verde
1 cup flat-leaf parsley leaves
1 cup mint leaves
1 tablespoon finely grated lemon rind
2 tablespoons lemon juice
1 tablespoon Dijon mustard
¼ cup (60ml) olive oil

Preheat oven to 200°C (400°F). Place the pastry on a baking tray lined with non-stick baking paper. Top with the feta and bake for 15–20 minutes or until golden.

To make the mint salsa verde, place the parsley, mint, lemon rind and juice, mustard and oil in a small food processor and process until finely chopped. Toss to combine half the salsa verde with the snow peas, sugar snaps and peas. Divide the pastry between plates, top with the salad, pea shoots and remaining salsa verde to serve. SERVES 4.

big vegetable curry puffs

4 sheets store-bought shortcrust pastry, thawed
1 egg, lightly beaten
vegetable filling
2 large starchy potatoes, peeled and chopped
250g butternut pumpkin (squash), peeled and chopped
250g sweet potato (kumara), peeled and chopped
1 tablespoon store-bought Thai red curry paste
1 cup (120g) frozen peas, thawed
½ cup (125ml) coconut milk
¼ cup chopped coriander (cilantro) leaves
¼ cup chopped mint leaves
sea salt and cracked black pepper
store-bought tzatziki*, to serve

Preheat oven to 180°C (350°F). To make the filling, steam the potato, pumpkin and sweet potato for 8–10 minutes or until tender. Place in a bowl with the curry paste, peas, coconut milk, coriander, mint, salt and pepper and mix to combine. Cut each pastry sheet in half diagonally. Place the filling on one side of each triangle and fold diagonally to enclose. Press the edges to seal. Place on baking trays lined with non-stick baking paper and brush with a little egg. Bake for 25–30 minutes or until golden. Serve with tzatziki. SERVES 4.

mint, zucchini and haloumi fritters

4 zucchinis (courgettes), grated
½ cup chopped mint leaves
5 eggs
¼ cup (40g) self-raising (self-rising) flour
sea salt and cracked black pepper
butter, for frying
500g haloumi*, sliced
olive oil, for brushing
2 vine-ripened tomatoes, sliced
1 cup mint leaves
lemon wedges, to serve

Place the zucchini, mint, eggs, flour, salt and pepper in a bowl and mix to combine. Melt a little butter in a non-stick frying pan over medium–high heat. Add spoonfuls of the zucchini mixture to the pan and cook, in batches, for 2–3 minutes each side or until golden. Set aside and keep warm.

Brush the haloumi with oil and cook, in batches, for 1–2 minutes each side or until golden. Serve the haloumi with the fritters, tomatoes, mint and lemon wedges. SERVES 4.

red curry roasted vegetables

Roasted carrots, beetroot and crispy leeks give this robust one-pan salad a lovely sweet kick.

roasted vegetable salad with buttermilk dressing

red curry roasted vegetables

2 small sweet potatoes (kumara), halved
4 large pieces pumpkin
2 zucchinis (courgettes), halved
2 tablespoons store-bought Thai red curry paste
⅓ cup (80ml) coconut cream
vegetable oil, for drizzling
basil and coriander (cilantro) leaves, thick natural yoghurt and
  steamed jasmine rice, to serve

Preheat oven to 200°C (400°F). Using a small sharp knife, score the flesh of the sweet potatoes, pumpkin and zucchinis and place on a baking tray lined with non-stick baking paper. Combine the curry paste and coconut cream and spread generously over the vegetables. Drizzle with a little oil and roast for 30–40 minutes or until the vegetables are soft. Divide between plates, top with basil and coriander and serve with steamed rice and yoghurt. SERVES 4.

roasted vegetable salad with buttermilk dressing

16 Dutch (baby) carrots, peeled and trimmed
5 baby leeks, trimmed and halved
12 baby beetroot, trimmed and halved
¼ cup (60ml) balsamic vinegar
2 tablespoons caster (superfine) sugar
2 tablespoons olive oil
8 slices char-grilled bread
rocket (arugula) leaves, to serve
½ cup (125ml) buttermilk
125g goat's curd*
sea salt and cracked black pepper

Preheat oven to 200°C (400°F). Place the carrots, leeks and beetroot in a bowl. Pour over the balsamic, sugar and oil and toss to combine. Place on a baking tray lined with non-stick baking paper and roast for 20–25 minutes or until the vegetables are just soft.

Divide the bread between plates and top with the roasted vegetables and rocket leaves. Mix to combine the buttermilk, goat's curd, salt and pepper and spoon over the vegetables. SERVES 4.

crispy pancetta, spinach and ricotta bake

26 slices round pancetta*
300g baby spinach leaves
2½ cups (500g) fresh ricotta
¼ cup chopped dill leaves
¼ cup chopped mint leaves
¼ cup chopped flat-leaf parsley leaves
4 eggs
½ cup (40g) finely grated parmesan
sea salt and cracked black pepper

Preheat oven to 180°C (350°F). Line the base and sides of a shallow ceramic ovenproof dish with 16 slices of the pancetta.

Place the spinach in a bowl, pour over boiling water, stand for 10 seconds and drain. Dry the spinach on absorbent paper and roughly chop. Place the spinach, ricotta, dill, mint, parsley, eggs, parmesan, salt and pepper in a bowl and mix to combine. Spoon the mixture into the pancetta-lined dish. Cover with remaining slices of pancetta and bake for 40 minutes or until filling is set and pancetta is crisp. Serve warm with a simple green salad, if desired. SERVES 4.

spiced sweet potato soup

1 tablespoon olive oil
2 teaspoons ground cumin
2 teaspoons ground coriander (cilantro)
2 teaspoons dried chilli flakes
1kg sweet potato (kumara), peeled and roughly grated
2 litres (8 cups) chicken or vegetable stock
¼ cup (35g) slivered almonds, toasted and chopped
coriander (cilantro) leaves and thick plain yoghurt, to serve

Heat the oil in a saucepan over medium heat. Add the cumin, ground coriander and chilli and cook for 2 minutes until fragrant. Add the sweet potato and stock and bring to the boil. Cover and simmer for 8 minutes or until sweet potato is soft. Divide between bowls and top with almonds and coriander and serve with the yoghurt. SERVES 4.

Using crisp, salty pancetta, this is my version of spinach and ricotta pie without the pastry.

crispy pancetta, spinach and ricotta bake

spiced sweet potato soup

tips & tricks

RIGHT
For a simple way to remove the seeds from cherry tomatoes, if using them in a sauce, place in a colander and press them with a masher.

BELOW
Use a vegetable peeler to get really long thin ribbons of cucumber, zucchini or carrot for an elegant salad.

I always keep a selection of seasonal vegetables in the crisper for a great base to a recipe, a quick salad or sides or a burst of fresh flavour in a pasta.

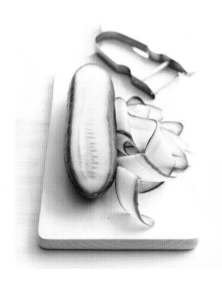

ABOVE
For a thin, crisp result in salads, it's best to shave fennel or other hard vegetables with a mandolin.

LEFT
To keep herbs fresh in the fridge, don't keep them in a plastic bag. Wrap them in a damp, clean tea towel and store in the crisper.

fruit

fig and brown sugar clafoutis

roasted strawberries and rhubarb with whipped mascarpone

fig and brown sugar clafoutis

½ cup (60g) almond meal (ground almonds)
1 tablespoon cornflour (cornstarch)
½ cup (110g) caster (superfine) sugar
2 eggs
1 egg yolk, extra
30g butter, melted
1 teaspoon vanilla extract
2 tablespoons single (pouring) cream*
4 fresh figs, halved
¼ cup (45g) brown sugar
icing (confectioner's) sugar, for dusting
vanilla ice-cream, to serve

Preheat oven to 170°C (350°F). Place the almond meal, cornflour and caster sugar in a bowl. Add the eggs, extra yolk, butter, vanilla and cream and whisk until smooth. Pour the mixture into 4 shallow 1-cup (250ml) capacity baking dishes. Press the cut side of the figs into the brown sugar and place the figs, cut-side up, into the batter. Bake for 30 minutes or until cooked when tested with a skewer. Dust with icing sugar and serve warm with ice-cream. SERVES 4.

The great thing about clafoutis is that you can use almost any soft fruit in the recipe. Try it with apricots or berries.

roasted strawberries and rhubarb with whipped mascarpone

600g strawberries, hulled
6 stalks rhubarb, trimmed and cut into 4
1 vanilla bean, split and seeds scraped
⅓ cup (55g) caster (superfine) sugar
¼ cup (60ml) balsamic vinegar
whipped mascarpone
250g mascarpone*
1¼ cups (250g) fresh ricotta
1 tablespoon icing (confectioner's) sugar
1 teaspoon vanilla extract

Preheat oven to 180°C (350°F). Place the strawberries, rhubarb, vanilla bean and seeds, caster sugar and vinegar in a bowl and toss to combine. Place on a baking tray lined with non-stick baking paper and roast for 15 minutes or until the fruit is soft.

To make the whipped mascarpone, place the mascarpone, ricotta, icing sugar and vanilla extract in a food processor and blend until smooth. Divide the fruit and pan juices between plates and serve with the whipped mascarpone. SERVES 4.

oven puff cake with blueberries

½ cup (75g) plain (all-purpose) flour, sifted
2 tablespoons caster (superfine) sugar
2 eggs
½ cup (125ml) milk
1 teaspoon vanilla extract
30g butter
blueberries and vanilla ice-cream, to serve
icing (confectioner's) sugar, for dusting

Preheat oven to 200°C (400°F). Place an 18cm heavy-based frying pan with an ovenproof handle into the oven and heat for 20 minutes. Place the flour and caster sugar in a bowl and make a well in the centre. Add the eggs, milk and vanilla and whisk until smooth. Using a pot holder, carefully take the pan out of the oven, add the butter and swirl until melted. Pour in the batter and place the pan back in the oven. Bake for 25 minutes or until the cake is puffed and golden. Top the cake with the blueberries, dust with icing sugar and serve warm with vanilla ice-cream. SERVES 4.

This fluffy puffed cake follows
the same concept as a Yorkshire
pudding, only much sweeter.

oven puff cake with blueberries

strawberry, lychee and mint granita

375g strawberries, hulled
1 x 565g can lychees in syrup
2 tablespoons caster (superfine) sugar
2 tablespoons finely chopped mint
⅓ cup (80ml) coconut cream, for drizzling

Place the strawberries, lychees, lychee syrup and sugar in a food processor and blend until smooth. Press the mixture through a sieve to remove the seeds. Stir through the mint, pour into a shallow metal container and freeze for 4 hours or until set. Rake the top of the granita with a fork, spoon into glasses and drizzle with a little coconut cream to serve. SERVES 4.

peach and raspberry coconut crumble

4 peaches, sliced and stones removed
125g fresh or frozen raspberries
2 tablespoons maple syrup
vanilla ice-cream, to serve
coconut crumble
1½ cups (110g) shredded coconut
⅔ cup (150g) caster (superfine) sugar
1 eggwhite

Preheat oven to 160°C (325°F). Divide the peaches and raspberries between 4 x 1-cup (250ml) capacity ovenproof dishes and drizzle with the maple syrup.

To make the coconut crumble, place the coconut, sugar and eggwhite in a bowl and mix to combine. Spoon the coconut mixture over the fruit and bake for 15–20 minutes or until the crumble is lightly browned. Serve warm with vanilla ice-cream. SERVES 4.

pistachio cakes with raspberries and rosewater cream

¾ cup (90g) almond meal (ground almonds)
⅓ cup (45g) unsalted shelled pistachios
125g butter, softened
1⅔ cups (270g) icing (confectioner's) sugar, sifted
½ cup (75g) plain (all-purpose) flour
½ teaspoon baking powder
5 eggwhites
1 cup fresh or frozen raspberries
1 cup (250ml) single (pouring) cream, whipped
1 tablespoon icing (confectioner's) sugar, sifted, extra
½ teaspoon rosewater*
extra pistachios, to serve

Preheat oven to 180°C (350°F). Place the almond meal and pistachios in a food processor and process until finely chopped. Add the butter, sugar, flour, baking powder and eggwhites and process until smooth. Pour the mixture into a 12 x ½-cup (125ml) capacity greased non-stick muffin tin. Top with the raspberries and bake for 20 minutes or until cakes are just cooked. Place the cream in a bowl and gently fold in the extra icing sugar and rosewater. Spoon on top of the cakes and sprinkle with extra pistachios to serve. MAKES 12.

caramelised apricots with brown sugar crème fraîche

12 apricots, halved and stones removed
1 vanilla bean, split and seeds scraped
¼ cup (55g) caster (superfine) sugar
½ cup (120g) crème fraîche*
1 tablespoon brown sugar

Place the apricots, vanilla bean and seeds in a bowl and toss to combine. Place, cut-side up, on a baking tray lined with non-stick baking paper. Sprinkle with the caster sugar and cook under a preheated hot grill (broiler) for 4 minutes or until the sugar has caramelised. Divide apricots between plates, spoon over the crème fraîche and sprinkle with brown sugar to serve. SERVES 4.

The tangy yoghurt and tart
passionfruit give this dessert
a lovely fresh summer flavour.

passionfruit yoghurt fool

cherries in wine syrup

passionfruit yoghurt fool

¾ cup (180ml) single (pouring) cream*
1 cup (280g) thick plain yoghurt
⅓ cup (55g) icing (confectioner's) sugar, sifted
⅓ cup passionfruit pulp (approximately 3 passionfruit), strained
extra passionfruit pulp, to serve

Place the cream, yoghurt and sugar in a bowl and whip until soft peaks form. Fold through the strained passionfruit pulp. Spoon into serving glasses and chill until ready to serve. Spoon over extra passionfruit pulp to serve. SERVES 4.

cherries in wine syrup

2½ cups (625ml) dessert wine+
½ cup (110g) white sugar
1 vanilla bean, split and seeds scraped
600g white or red cherries, stalks removed
vanilla ice-cream, to serve

Place the wine, sugar and vanilla bean and seeds in a saucepan over medium–low heat and simmer for 5–7 minutes or until thick and syrupy. Add the cherries and simmer for 2 minutes. Remove from heat and stand for 5 minutes. Serve the cherries warm or chilled with vanilla ice-cream. SERVES 4.
+ You can use a Sauterne-style wine or botrytis-affected dessert wine in this recipe. The cherries will keep in the fridge for 3 days.

This is the perfect grown-up dessert that is equally good served plain with chocolate ice-cream or as part of a trifle.

lemon curd and raspberry brioche pudding

8 slices brioche*
½ cup (175g) store-bought lemon curd
150g fresh or frozen raspberries
¾ cup (180ml) single (pouring) cream*
¾ cup (180ml) milk
1 teaspoon vanilla extract
2 tablespoons caster sugar
3 eggs
white sugar, extra, for sprinkling
icing (confectioner's) sugar, for dusting
vanilla ice-cream, to serve

Preheat oven to 180°C (350°F). Spread one side of the brioche slices with the lemon curd and place in a 1.5-litre capacity baking dish. Sprinkle with the raspberries, allowing some to fall between the layers of brioche. Place the cream, milk, vanilla, caster sugar and eggs in a bowl and whisk to combine. Pour the egg mixture over the brioche, sprinkle with the extra sugar and cover with aluminium foil. Bake for 20 minutes, uncover and bake for a further 15 minutes or until pudding is just set and golden. Stand for 5 minutes, dust with icing sugar and serve with vanilla ice-cream. SERVES 4.

banoffee pie

150g plain sweet shortbread biscuits, crushed
100g butter, melted
150g dark chocolate, chopped
¼ cup (60ml) single (pouring) cream*
½ cup store-bought caramel filling or dulce de leche*
1 cup (250ml) double (thick) cream*
2 tablespoons icing (confectioner's) sugar
1 cup (280g) sour cream
3 bananas, peeled and thinly sliced

Combine the biscuits and butter and press into the base and sides of a 24cm pie dish. Refrigerate until chilled. Place the chocolate and single cream in a saucepan over low heat and stir until smooth. Pour the chocolate over the chilled base and spread with the back of a spoon to coat the base evenly. Refrigerate for 5 minutes. Pour the caramel over the base.
   Place the double cream, icing sugar and sour cream in a bowl and whip until soft peaks form. Gently fold the bananas through ¾ of the cream mixture and spoon over the caramel layer. Top with remaining cream mixture and chill until ready to serve. SERVES 6–8.

lemon curd and raspberry brioche pudding

This pie is proof that chocolate, banana and luscious caramel were meant to be together.

banoffee pie

tips & tricks

Frozen fruit is great to buy when berries are out of season. When using it in baking or desserts, you don't need to thaw it first.

Even liquid fruits can be stored for future use. Passionfruit pulp, lemon or lime juice can be frozen into handy ice cubes.

I love eating fruit that's sweet and in season, but when it's in such abundance, it would be a shame not to freeze it for baking and cooking.

Mango season is way too short! To make it last, scoop out the whole cheeks with a spoon and freeze. You'll be surprised by how much of their fragrance they retain.

When choosing seasonal fruit, follow your nose. Ripe berries and stonefruit should smell exquisite and sweet and be vibrant in colour.

chocolate

cheat's chocolate and salted caramel tarts

You don't even need an ice-cream machine to make this deliciously smooth and rich frozen treat.

chocolate semifreddo

cheat's chocolate and salted caramel tarts

12 thin plain round chocolate biscuits
¼ cup store-bought caramel filling or dulce de leche*
sea salt flakes, to serve
dark chocolate filling
200g dark chocolate, chopped
½ cup (125ml) single (pouring) cream*

Preheat oven to 140°C (275°F). Place the biscuits into a 12 x 30ml capacity lightly greased shallow patty tin. Bake for 5 minutes or until soft. Using a clean tea towel, press the biscuits into the tin to form a shell and allow to cool.

To make the chocolate filling, place the chocolate and cream in a saucepan over low heat and stir until smooth. Spoon filling into the biscuit shells and refrigerate until firm. Top the tarts with the caramel and sprinkle with a little sea salt to serve. MAKES 12.

This perfect cheat's dessert uses plain biscuits to create shells for the tarts. You could use them as a base for any filling.

chocolate semifreddo

3 eggs
2 egg yolks, extra
¾ cup (165g) caster (superfine) sugar
250g dark chocolate, melted
1¾ cups (430ml) single (pouring) cream*
2 tablespoons cocoa, sifted

Place the eggs, extra yolks and sugar into a heatproof bowl over a saucepan of simmering water. Using a hand-held electric mixer, beat for 6–8 minutes or until the mixture is pale and thick and doubled in volume.

Remove from the heat and continue beating until cool. Gently fold through the melted chocolate. Whip the cream until soft peaks form and fold through the cocoa. Gently fold the cream through the egg mixture, pour into a metal container, cover and freeze for 3–4 hours or until set. Spoon into glasses and serve with fresh berries, if desired. SERVES 4–6.

dark chocolate sorbet

2¾ cups (680ml) water
1 cup (220g) caster (superfine) sugar
½ cup (90g) brown sugar
1 cup (80g) good-quality cocoa, sifted

Place the water and both sugars in a saucepan over high heat and stir until the sugar is dissolved and the mixture begins to boil. Reduce heat to medium, add the cocoa and whisk until smooth. Allow the mixture to rapidly simmer for 14–17 minutes, stirring occasionally, until the mixture is thick and syrupy and reaches 96°C (200°F) on a sugar thermometer. Allow the mixture to cool and churn in an ice-cream machine according to manufacturer's instructions. Freeze until ready to serve. SERVES 4.

dark chocolate sorbet

molten chocolate puddings

185g butter
185g dark chocolate, chopped
4 eggs
¾ cup (165g) brown sugar
¾ cup (115g) self-raising (self-rising) flour, sifted
vanilla ice-cream, to serve

Preheat oven to 180°C (350°F). Place the butter and chocolate in a saucepan over low heat and stir until smooth. Pour the chocolate into a bowl and add the eggs, sugar and flour and whisk to combine. Pour the mixture into 6 x 1-cup (250ml) capacity ramekins and place in a baking dish. Pour in enough boiling water to come half way up the sides of the ramekins. Bake for 45 minutes or until the puddings are just set. Serve with vanilla ice-cream. SERVES 6.

chocolate meringue mess

100g dark chocolate, chopped
¼ cup (60ml) single (pouring) cream*
2 tablespoons coffee or chocolate liqueur
6 store-bought vanilla meringues
1 cup (250ml) single (pouring) cream*, extra, whipped

Place the chocolate, cream and liqueur in a saucepan over low heat and stir until smooth. Set aside to cool. Break the meringues into large pieces and divide evenly between serving glasses. Spoon over the whipped cream and top with the chocolate sauce. Serve with berries, if desired. SERVES 6.

cookies and cream ice-cream sandwiches

1 litre good-quality vanilla ice-cream
150g chocolate cream-filled biscuits, crushed
16 chocolate-coated plain sweet biscuits

Place the ice-cream in the bowl of an electric mixer and beat until soft. Fold though the crushed biscuits, pour into a metal container and freeze for 3 hours or until firm. Place a scoop of ice-cream onto a biscuit and sandwich with another biscuit to serve. MAKES 8.

espresso granita with bitter chocolate cream

2 cups (500ml) strong coffee
¾ cup (165g) caster (superfine) sugar
bitter chocolate cream
100g dark chocolate (70% cocoa solids), chopped
1 cup (250ml) single (pouring) cream*

To make the granita, place the coffee and sugar into a bowl and stir to dissolve the sugar. Pour into a shallow metal container and freeze for 4 hours or until frozen.

To make the bitter chocolate cream, place the chocolate and cream in a small saucepan over low heat and stir until smooth. Spoon into 4 serving glasses. Rake the top of the granita with a fork and scoop over the bitter chocolate cream. Serve immediately. SERVES 4.

baked chocolate and raspberry custards

easy chocolate mousse

baked chocolate and raspberry custards

125g dark chocolate, chopped
1 cup (250ml) milk
1 cup (250ml) single (pouring) cream*
2 eggs
2 egg yolks, extra
½ cup (90g) brown sugar
¾ cup raspberries, plus extra, to serve
cocoa, for dusting

Preheat oven to 150°C (300°F). Place the chocolate, milk and cream in a saucepan over medium heat and stir until the chocolate has melted and the mixture is hot but not boiling.

Place the eggs, extra yolks and sugar in a bowl and whisk until well combined. Slowly add the hot chocolate mixture and whisk to combine. Divide the raspberries between 4 x 1-cup (250ml) capacity ramekins and pour over the chocolate mixture. Place the ramekins in a baking dish and pour in enough hot water to come half way up the sides of the ramekins. Bake for 35 minutes or until the custard is just set. Top with extra raspberries, dust with cocoa and serve warm or cold. SERVES 4.

easy chocolate mousse

400g dark chocolate, chopped
1⅓ cups (330ml) milk
1½ tablespoons icing (confectioner's) sugar

Place the chocolate, milk and sugar in a saucepan over low heat and stir until smooth. Pour the chocolate mixture into a bowl and place over a larger bowl of ice. Using a hand-held electric mixer, beat for approximately 6 minutes or until light and fluffy. Do not overbeat the mixture or the mousse will be grainy. Spoon into glasses and serve immediately. SERVES 4.

You don't even need eggs to make this instant cheat's mousse. Simply beat the ingredients over ice until fluffy and serve. Too easy!

milk chocolate panna cotta

2 tablespoons water
2 teaspoons powdered gelatine
2 cups (500ml) single (pouring) cream*
⅓ cup (55g) brown sugar
100g milk chocolate, chopped
vegetable oil, for greasing
mixed berries, to serve

Place the water in a bowl, sprinkle over the gelatine and set aside until the gelatine is dissolved. Place the cream, sugar and chocolate in a saucepan over low heat and stir until smooth and hot. Add the gelatine mixture and stir well to combine. Pour the mixture into 4 x ½-cup (125ml) capacity lightly greased moulds or ramekins. Refrigerate for 4 hours or until firm. Unmold the panna cottas or serve in ramekins with mixed berries. SERVES 4.

individual chocolate bombe alaskas

6 store-bought uniced chocolate cupcakes
175ml dark chocolate ice-cream
1 tablespoon chocolate or coffee liqueur
3 eggwhites
¾ cup (165g) caster (superfine) sugar

Using a small knife, cut the centres from the cupcakes and scoop out the cake. Make a lid for each cake by cutting a thin slice from the top of the removed cakes. Drizzle the inside of the cakes with a little liqueur and fill with the ice-cream. Top with the reserved cake lids and freeze until firm.

Place the eggwhites in the bowl of an electric mixer and whisk until soft peaks form. Gradually add the sugar and whisk until the mixture is thick and glossy. Spread the meringue mixture over the cakes to completely cover. Place the cakes under a preheated hot grill (broiler) and cook for 1 minute or until the meringue is golden. Serve immediately. SERVES 6.

Combined with the chocolate, the brown sugar in this wobbly dessert gives it a caramelly flavour.

milk chocolate panna cotta

individual chocolate bombe alaskas

tips & tricks

RIGHT
There are two types of cocoa powder used in cooking: bitter and robust natural cocoa (left) and the more delicately flavoured Dutch cocoa (right).

BELOW
The secret to melting chocolate in the microwave is to heat it on a medium or low setting for short 1 minute bursts until fully melted.

Cooking with chocolate is easy once you have a little know-how and tips on melting and baking with this seriously addictive sweet.

ABOVE
Milk chocolate has a subtle and sweet flavour because it has fewer cocoa solids and more sugar. Dark chocolate has a rich, bitter flavour because it has more cocoa.

LEFT
You can only melt chocolate over direct heat when cream or butter has been added. Otherwise melt it in a heatproof bowl over a saucepan of simmering water.

glossary & index

Most of the ingredients in this book are
sourced from supermarkets, but if you're
unsure of a particular ingredient, you'll find
it in the glossary. Ingredients marked with
an asterisk are listed. Also included is basic
information on some staple ingredients.

There's also a useful list of global measures,
temperatures and common conversions.
To make recipes easier to find in the book,
they are listed alphabetically in the index
as well as by ingredient and theme, such
as soups, salads, pasta and so on.

aïoli

Garlic-flavoured mayonnaise.

almonds

meal

Also known as ground almonds, almond meal is available from most supermarkets. Make your own by processing whole skinned almonds to a fine meal in a food processor or blender (125g almonds will give 1 cup almond meal). To remove the skins from almonds, soak in boiling water, then, using your fingers, slip the skins off.

baba ghanoush

A creamy Middle Eastern dip of pureéd roasted eggplant, garlic, lemon juice, cumin and tahini (sesame seed paste) commonly served on a mezze platter with flat bread, for dipping. It has a distinct smoky flavour.

brioche

This sweet style of light and fluffy French yeast bread is enriched with plenty of butter and eggs, which give it a decadent airy texture. Commonly used for French toast.

butter

Unless stated otherwise in a recipe, butter should be at room temperature for cooking. It should not be half-melted or too soft to handle, but should still have some 'give' when pressed. When using butter for pastry, it should be cold and chopped into small pieces so that it can be evenly distributed through the flour. Salted butter has a longer refrigerator shelf life.

butter beans

Large, plump white beans also known as lima beans. They go well in soups, stews and salads. Available from delicatessens and supermarkets either canned or in dried form. Dried beans need to be soaked overnight in water before cooking.

capers

Capers are the small, green flower buds of the caper bush. Available packed either in brine or salt. Use salt-packed capers when possible, as the texture is firmer and the flavour superior. Before use, rinse thoroughly, drain and pat dry.

celeriac (celery root)

A root vegetable with white flesh and a mild celery flavour. It is available in winter from supermarkets and greengrocers. Use in salads and soups or roast it with meats.

caramelised onion relish

Sliced onion cooked slowly to release all its sugars and made even more intense in flavour by the addition of brown sugar and balsamic vinegar. It is sold as relish in most supermarkets.

cheese

blue

The distinctive veins and flavour of blue cheeses are achieved by adding a cultured mould. Most have a crumbly texture and acidic taste, which becomes rounded and more mellow with age.

bocconcini

Small, bite-sized balls of mozzarella.

goat's cheese & curd

Goat's milk has a tart flavour, so cheese made from it, sometimes labelled 'chèvre', has a sharp, slightly acidic taste. Immature goat's cheese is milder and creamier than mature cheese and is sometimes found labelled 'goat's curd'.

gorgonzola

Blue cheese of Italian origin. Dolce refers to an extra creamy sweet version.

gruyère

Firm cow's milk cheese with a smooth ivory interior and a natural brushed rind. Popular in Switzerland as a table cheese and cooked in fondues, gratins and quiches.

haloumi

Firm white Cypriot cheese made from sheep's milk. It has a stringy texture and is usually sold in brine. Available from delicatessens and some supermarkets. Holds its shape during grilling and frying, so is ideal for kebabs.

labne

Middle Eastern cheese made from strained yoghurt based on cow's milk.

manchego

Firm ivory-yellow cheese of Spanish origin made from sheep's milk.

mascarpone

A fresh Italian triple-cream, curd-style cheese. It has a similar consistency to thick (double) cream and is often used in the same way. Available in tubs from speciality food stores and supermarkets, it's used in sauces and desserts such as tiramisu.

mozzarella

Italian in origin, mozzarella is the mild cheese of pizza, lasagne and tomato salads. It's made by cutting and spinning (or stringing) the curd to achieve a smooth, elastic consistency. The most prized variety is made from buffalo milk. Bocconcini are small, bite-sized balls of mozzarella.

parmesan

Italy's favourite hard, granular cheese is made from cow's milk. Parmigiano reggiano is the 'Rolls-Royce' variety, made under strict guidelines in the Emilia-Romagna region and aged for an average of two years. Grana padano mainly comes from Lombardy and is aged for 15 months.

ricotta

A creamy, finely grained white cheese. Ricotta means 'recooked' in Italian, a reference to the way the cheese is produced by heating the whey left over from making other cheese varieties. It's fresh and creamy and low in fat.

chickpeas (garbanzos)

A legume native from western Asia across the Mediterranean, the chickpea is used in soups, stews and is the base ingredient in the Middle Eastern dip called hummus. Dried chickpeas must be soaked before cooking, but you can also buy them canned.

chillies

There are over 200 different types of chilli in the world. By general rule of thumb, long red or green chillies are milder, fruitier and sweeter, while small chillies are much hotter. Remove the membranes and seeds for a milder result in a dish.

chilli jam

Thai condiment made from ginger, chilli, garlic and shrimp paste used in soups and stir-fries. It goes well with roasted meats, egg dishes and cheese and is often served in a dollop as a garnish.

chinese five-spice powder

A blend of cinnamon, Sichuan pepper, star anise, clove and fennel seeds. Available at Asian food stores and supermarkets.

chinese cooking wine or shaoxing

Similar to dry sherry, Shaoxing or Chinese cooking wine is a blend of glutinous rice, millet, a special yeast and the local spring waters of Shao Hsing, where it is made, in northern China. It is sold in the Asian aisle of your supermarket and in Asian grocery stores, often labelled 'Shao Hsing'.

chorizo

Firm, spicy, coarse-textured Spanish pork sausage seasoned with pepper, paprika and chillies. Available fresh and dried from some butchers and most delicatessens. The dried variety is used in this book.

coconut

cream

The cream that rises to the top after the first pressing of coconut milk, coconut cream is a rich, sweet liquid that is both higher in energy and fat than regular coconut milk. A common ingredient in curries and Asian sweets.

milk

A milky sweet white liquid made by soaking grated fresh coconut flesh or desiccated coconut in warm water and squeezing through muslin or cheesecloth to extract the liquid. Available in cans or freeze-dried from supermarkets, coconut milk should not be confused with coconut juice, which is a clear liquid found inside young coconuts and often served as a refreshing drink in Asia.

coriander (cilantro)

Also known as Chinese parsley, this pungent green herb is common in Asian and Mexican cooking. The finely chopped roots are sometimes incorporated in curry pastes. The dried seeds are an Indian staple, sold ground or whole and one of the base ingredients in curry powder. The dried form can not be substituted for fresh.

couscous

The name given to both the national dish of Algeria, Tunisia and Morocco and the tiny grains of flour-coated semolina that make it.

cream

The fat content determines the names of the different types of cream and their uses.

crème fraîche

A fermented cream with a minimum fat content of 35 per cent and a tangy flavour.

double (heavy)

Has a butter fat content of 40–50 per cent. It is usually served on the side of warm puddings or rich cakes.

single (pouring)

Has a butter fat content of 20–30 per cent. It is the type of cream most commonly used for making ice-cream, panna cotta and custard. It can be whipped to a light and airy consistency. Often called pure cream or whipping cream.

sour

A thick, commercially cultured cream with a minimum fat content of 35 per cent.

thickened

This is single (pouring) cream that has had a vegetable gum added to stabilise it. The gum makes the cream a little thicker and easier to whip. It's ideal for desserts and pavlovas.

dijon mustard

Also known as French mustard, this is a pale, creamy and fairly mild-flavoured mustard.

dulce de leche

This is a thick milk caramel made from slowly heating and thickening sweetened milk. You can buy it in cans or make your own by boiling an unopened can of sweetened condensed milk (not a ring-pull can) for 2–3 hours. It's used in desserts.

eggs

The standard egg size used in this book is 60g. It is important to use the right size eggs for a recipe, as this will affect the outcome of baked goods. The correct volume is especially important when using eggwhites to make meringues. You should use eggs at room temperature for baking.

fennel

With a mild aniseed flavour and crisp texture, fennel bulb is ideal for salads or roasting with meat and fish.

fish sauce

An amber-coloured liquid drained from salted fermented fish and used to add flavour to Thai and Vietnamese dishes such as curries and in dressings for salads. There are different grades available.

flat bread

There are many types of Middle Eastern flat breads available, from small or large round pide or Lebanese bread, which can act as 'pockets' for fillings, to long loaves of Afghan and Turkish bread.

flour

Made from ground cereal grains, flour is the primary ingredient in breads, cakes and many other baked goods including biscuits, pastries, pizzas and pie cases.

cornflour (cornstarch)

When made from ground corn or maize, cornflour is a gluten-free flour. It is often blended with water or stock to use as a thickening agent. Not to be confused with cornflour in the United States, which is finely ground corn meal.

plain (all-purpose)

Ground from the endosperm of wheat, plain white flour contains no raising agent.

self-raising (self-rising)

Ground from the endosperm of wheat, self-raising flour contains raising agents including sodium carbonates and calcium phosphates. To make it using plain flour add 2 teaspoons of baking powder for every 250g of flour.

rice

A fine flour made from ground white rice. Used as a thickening agent, in baking and to coat foods when cooking Asian dishes, particularly those needing a crispy finish. Buy from supermarkets.

gai larn

Also known as Chinese broccoli or Chinese kale, gai larn is a leafy vegetable with dark green leaves, small flowers and stout stems.

gelatine

Available as a powder or in leaf form, gelatine is a setting agent made from collagen. It must be dissolved in warm water before being added to the recipe. Agar-agar is a vegetarian alternative.

gowgee wrappers

Chinese in origin, these square thin sheets of dough are available fresh or frozen. They can be steamed or fried. Fill them with meat, vegetables and herbs to make dumplings for soup, or use as a crunchy base for nibbles, or deep-fry and sprinkle with sugar for dessert.

green mango

Green version of the tropical fruit with a strong sour taste, used in Asian salads.

green onion (scallion)

Both the white and green part of this small bulbed, mild onion are used in salads, as a garnish and in Asian cooking.

harissa

A North African condiment, harissa is a hot red paste made from chilli, garlic and spices including coriander, caraway and cumin. May also contain tomato. Available in jars and tubes from supermarkets and speciality food stores, harissa enlivens tagines and couscous dishes and can be added to dressings and sauces for an instant flavour kick. You can also use it in a marinade for meats.

horseradish

A pungent root vegetable that releases mustard oil when cut or grated. Available fresh from greengrocers or in jars from the supermarket. Commonly sold as grated horseradish or horseradish cream. A superb partner for pork and roast beef.

kaffir lime leaves

Fragrant leaves with a distinctive, double-leaf structure, used crushed or shredded in Thai dishes. Available fresh or dried from Asian food stores.

kecap manis

An Indonesian soy sauce sweetened with palm sugar. Thicker and sweeter than normal soy sauce. Commonly used in stir-fries and noodle dishes.

lemongrass

A tall, lemon-scented grass used in Asian cooking, and particularly in Thai dishes. Peel away the outer leaves and chop the tender white root-end finely, or add in large pieces during cooking and remove before serving. If adding in large pieces, bruise them with the back of a large knife.

maple syrup

A sweetener made from the sap of the maple tree. Be sure to use pure maple syrup rather than imitation or pancake syrup, which is made from corn syrup flavoured with maple and does not have the same intensity of flavour.

mirin

A Japanese pale yellow cooking wine made from glutinous rice and alcohol. Sweet mirin is flavoured with corn syrup.

miso paste

A traditional Japanese ingredient produced by fermenting rice, barley or soybeans, with salt and fungus to a thick paste. Used for sauces and spreads, pickling vegetables or meats, and mixing with dashi soup stock to serve as miso soup. Red miso paste is robust while white miso paste is more delicate in flavour. Available from supermarkets and Asian food stores.

mizuna

A type of Japanese lettuce with feathery, delicate leaves and a mild peppery flavour. A very decorative lettuce.

noodles

Keep a supply of dried noodles in the pantry for last-minute meals. Fresh noodles will keep in the fridge for a week. Available from supermarkets and Asian food stores.

cellophane (bean thread)

Also called mung bean vermicelli or glass noodles, these noodles are very thin and almost transparent. Soak them in boiling water and drain well to prepare for use.

dried rice

Fine, dry noodles that are common in Southeast Asian cooking. Depending on their thickness, rice noodles need only be boiled briefly, or soaked in hot water until soft and pliable.

rice vermicelli

Very thin dried rice noodles sometimes called rice sticks. They are usually used in soups such as laksa and in salads.

shanghai or singapore

Chinese wheat noodles available dried and fresh in a variety of thicknesses. Fresh noodles need to be soaked in hot water or cooked in boiling water. Dried noodles should be boiled before use.

soba

Japanese noodles made from buckwheat and wheat flour, soba are greyish brown in colour and served both hot and cold.

olives

black

Black olives are more mature and less salty than the green variety. Choose firm olives with good colour and a fruity taste.

kalamata

Of Greek origin, the large Kalamata olives have an intense flavour, which makes them the ideal choice for Greek salads. They are sometimes sold split to better absorb the flavour of the oil in which they are stored.

ligurian/wild

Usually labelled or sold as Ligurian olives, wild olives are uncultivated and grow close to the ground in clusters. This small variety of olive can range in colour from pale mustard to dark purple and black. The thin flesh has a nutty flavour that makes them a great substitute for peanuts. Niçoise olives are similar in size as well as flavour.

oil

Olive oil is graded according to its flavour, aroma and acidity. Extra virgin is the highest quality oil; it contains no more than 1 per cent acid. Virgin is the next best; it contains 1.5 per cent or less acid and may have a slightly fruitier taste than extra virgin. Bottles labelled 'olive oil' contain a combination of refined and unrefined virgin olive oil. Light olive oil is the least pure in quality and intensity of flavour; it is not lower in fat. Colours vary from deep green through to gold and very light yellow.

tapenade

Paste made by blending olives, capers, garlic and anchovies with oil. Served as a dip with crackers, or spread on bruschetta and pizzas, it makes a good marinade and partner for cold meat or cheeses.

pancetta

A cured Italian meat that is like prosciutto but less salty and with a softer texture. It's sold as round pancetta that has been rolled and is then sliced, perfect for an antipasto platter or grilled until crispy and added to salad, pasta or risotto. Also sold as an unrolled piece or chunk called flat pancetta, which you can chop and use like other cured pork products such as speck or bacon.

pasta

fettucine

Ribbon pasta available fresh and dried.

orecchiette

Small disc-shaped pasta that gets its name from the Italian for 'little ears'.

pappardelle

Thick ribbon pasta available fresh and dried. Ideal for chunky sauces.

penne

Pasta tubes, sometimes with a serrated edge, that's ideal for sauce to cling to.

rigatoni

Large grooved tube-shaped pasta.

spaghetti

Long thin strands of pasta available fresh and dried. Also comes as a thinner spaghetti that cooks faster and is sometimes called 'angel hair' pasta.

pastry

filo

Extremely thin sheets of pastry popular in Greek, Turkish and Middle Eastern baking, particularly for sweets.

puff

This pastry is time-consuming and quite difficult to make, so many cooks opt to use store-bought puff pastry. It can be bought in blocks from pâtisseries or bought in both block and sheet forms from supermarkets. You may need to layer several sheets of puff pastry together to make a thicker crown. It's perfect for quick tarts or desserts.

shortcrust

A savoury or sweet pastry that is available ready-made in blocks and frozen sheets. Keep a supply for last-minute pies or make your own pastry:

1½ cups (225g) plain (all-purpose) flour
125g butter, chilled and cut into cubes
3 egg yolks
1 tablespoon iced water

Place the flour and butter in the bowl of a food processor and process in short bursts until mixture resembles fine breadcrumbs. While the motor is running, add the egg yolks and water. Process until the dough just comes together. Turn dough out onto a lightly floured surface and gently bring together to form a ball. Using your hands, flatten dough into a disc. Wrap in plastic wrap and refrigerate. When ready to use, roll out on a lightly floured surface to 3mm thick. To make sweet shortcrust pastry, add ½ cup (80g) icing (confectioner's) sugar.

pistachio

A green delicately flavoured nut inside a hard outer shell. Used in Middle Eastern cuisine, salads and baking.

polenta

Used extensively in northern Italy, this corn meal is cooked in simmering water until it has a porridge-like consistency. In this form it is enriched with butter or cheese and served with meat dishes. Otherwise it is left to cool, cut into squares and grilled, fried or baked. Instant polenta is made from precooked corn meal and is ready in 5 minutes.

porcini mushrooms

Available fresh in Europe and the UK and sold dried elsewhere, including Australia and the US. They have an almost meaty texture and earthy taste. Soak dried porcini mushrooms before using, and use the soaking liquid if desired.

preserved lemon

Preserved lemons are rubbed with salt, packed in jars, covered with lemon juice and left for about four weeks. They're often flavoured with cloves, cinnamon or chilli. Remove the flesh, rinse and chop the rind for use in cooking. They are popular in Moroccan cuisine, where they are added to tagines. Available from delicatessens and speciality food stores.

prosciutto

Italian ham that's been salted and dried for up to two years. The paper-thin slices are eaten raw or used to lend their distinctive flavour to braises and other cooked dishes. Often used to wrap figs or melon as part of an antipasto platter.

quince paste

Also known as membrillo for its Spanish origins, this intensely aromatic paste is made by boiling quinces, lemon juice and sugar to a thick condiment that teams well with roasted meats, cheeses and nuts. Also delicious with roasted pork.

rice

arborio

Risotto rice with a short, plump-looking grain. It has surface starch which creates a cream with the stock when cooked to al dente. Substitute with carnaroli, roma, baldo, padano, vialone or Calriso rice.

basmati

Long-grain, aromatic white rice. Often used in Indian cooking and perfect to serve with curries.

jasmine

Sometimes called Thai rice, a long-grain white rice with a delicate floral flavour.

red curry paste

Buy good-quality pastes in jars from Asian food stores or the supermarket. You can buy Indian or Thai-style curry pastes. When trying a new brand, it is a good idea to add a little at a time to test the heat as the chilli intensity can vary significantly from brand to brand.

rocket (arugula)

A tangy, peppery salad leaf popular in Mediterranean cuisines, rocket makes a classic Italian salad with pear and parmesan, and also makes a great pesto to serve on bruschetta, in soups and as a dip.

rosewater

An essence distilled from rose petals, rosewater is one of the cornerstone flavours of Indian, Middle Eastern and Turkish tables. It's the distinctive flavour in Turkish delight and other sweet pastries.

sauces

hoisin

A thick, sweet Chinese sauce made from fermented soybeans, sugar, salt and red rice. Used as a dipping sauce or marinade and as the sauce for Peking duck, hoisin is available in supermarkets.

oyster

A viscous dark brown sauce commonly used in Asian stir-fries, soups and hotpots, oyster sauce is made from oysters, brine and flavour enhancers, which are boiled until reduced to a thick, caramelised, flavour-packed sauce.

worcestershire

A thin, dark brown sauce developed by the British in India, with strong overtones of tamarind and spice. Used to give a kick to soups, stews and oysters Kilpatrick.

sesame seeds

These small seeds have a strong nutty flavour. White sesame seeds are the most common variety, but black, or unhulled, seeds are popular for coatings in Asian cooking. Sesame oil is made by extracting the oil from roasted seeds.

smoked paprika

Unlike Hungarian paprika, the Spanish style known as pimentón is deep and smoky in flavour. It is made from smoked, ground pimiento peppers and comes in varying intensities from sweet and mild (dulce), bittersweet medium hot (agridulce) and hot (picante).

star anise

Small, brown seed-cluster that is shaped like a star. It has a strong aniseed flavour and can be used whole or ground in sweet and savoury dishes.

sugar

Extracted as crystals from the juice of the sugar cane plant or beet, sugar is a sweetener, flavour enhancer, bulking agent and preservative.

brown

Processed with molasses. It comes in differing shades of brown, according to the quantity of molasses added, which varies between countries. This also affects the taste of the sugar, and therefore the end product. Brown sugar is sometimes called light brown sugar. You can substitute dark brown sugar for more intense flavour.

caster (superfine)

Gives baked products a light texture and crumb, which is important for many cakes and light desserts such as meringues.

demerara

Small-grained, golden-coloured crystal sugar used in baking.

granulated

Regular sugar is used in baking when a light texture is not crucial. The crystals are large, so you need to beat, add liquids or heat regular sugar to dissolve it.

icing (confectioner's)

Regular granulated sugar ground to a very fine powder. It often clumps together and needs to be sieved before using. Use pure icing sugar not icing sugar mixture, which contains cornflour (cornstarch) and needs more liquid.

sumac

Dried berries of a flowering plant are ground to produce an acidic, reddish-purple powder popular in the Middle East.

sweet potato (kumara)

Long, tuberous root available in white- and orange-fleshed varieties. The orange sweet potato, also known as kumara, is sweeter and moister than the white. Both varieties can be roasted, boiled or mashed. Although different from the yam, they can be cooked in a similar manner.

swiss chard

Also known as silverbeet, this spinach has deep green leaves and also comes in a coloured variety with a pretty rhubarb hue.

tahini

A thick paste made from ground sesame seeds. Used in Middle Eastern cooking, it is available in jars and cans from supermarkets and health food shops. It is used to make the popular dip hummus.

tarragon

Called the king of herbs by the French and used in many of their classic sauces such as Béarnaise and tartare. It has a slightly aniseed flavour.

tins

Aluminium (aluminum) tins are fine but stainless steel will last longer and won't warp or buckle. Always measure widths across the base of the tin.

muffin

The standard sizes are a 12-hole tin, each hole with ½ cup (125ml) capacity, or a 6-hole tin, each hole with 1 cup (250ml) capacity. Mini-muffin tins have a capacity of 1½ tablespoons. Non-stick tins make for easy removal, or line with paper cases.

round

The standard sizes for round tins are 18cm, 20cm, 22cm and 24cm. The 20cm and 24cm tins are must-haves.

springform

The standard sizes for springform tins are 18cm, 20cm, 22cm and 24cm. The 20cm and 24cm round tins are the must-have members of the range.

square

The standard sizes for square tins are 18cm, 20cm, 22cm and 24cm. If you have a recipe for a cake cooked in a round tin and you want to use a square tin, the general rule is to subtract 2cm from the size of the tin. For example, you would need a 20cm square tin for a recipe calling for a 22cm round cake tin.

tofu

Literally translated as 'bean curd', tofu is made by coagulating the milk of soy beans, and pressing the curd into blocks. Tofu comes in several grades according to the amount of moisture which has been removed. Silken tofu is the softest, with a custard-like texture. Soft tofu is slightly firmer, while dried or firm tofu has the texture of, and cuts like, a semi-hard cheese such as haloumi. Usually sold in the refrigerated section of supermarkets.

tomato

bottled tomato pasta sauce

Sometimes labelled 'passata' or 'sugo'. Italian for 'passed', passata is made by removing the skins and seeds from ripe tomatoes and passing the flesh through a sieve to make a thick, rich, pulpy tomato purée. Sugo is made from crushed tomatoes so it has a little more texture than passata. Both are available in bottles from supermarkets.

paste

Triple-concentrated tomato purée used to flavour soups, sauces and stews.

purée

Canned puréed tomatoes (not tomato paste). Substitute with fresh or canned peeled and puréed tomatoes.

sun-dried

Tomato pieces that have been dried with salt, which dehydrates the fruit and concentrates the flavour. Available plain or packed in oil. These are great chopped into salads or pastas for an extra tomato flavour boost.

tzatziki

Greek dip made from thick natural yoghurt, garlic and chopped or grated cucumber, sometimes with dill added. Available in supermarkets, it can also be used as a sauce for grilled meat and seafood or served as an accompaniment to savoury pastries.

vanilla beans

These cured pods from the vanilla orchid are used whole, and often split with the tiny seeds inside scraped into the mixture, to infuse flavour into custard and cream-based recipes. If unavailable, substitute 1 vanilla bean with 1 teaspoon pure vanilla extract (a dark, thick liquid – not essence) or store-bought vanilla bean paste.

vanilla extract

For a pure vanilla taste, use a good-quality vanilla extract, not an essence or imitation flavour, or use a fresh vanilla bean.

vinegar

balsamic

Originally from Modena in Italy, there are many varieties on the market ranging in quality and flavour. Aged balsamics are generally preferable. Also available in a milder, white version which is used in dishes where the colour is important.

balsamic glaze

A thick and syrupy reduction of balsamic vinegar and sugar.

malt

A brown vinegar made from fermented malt and beech shavings.

rice wine

Made from fermenting rice or rice wine, rice vinegar is milder and sweeter than vinegars made by oxidising distilled alcohol or wine made from grapes. Rice wine

vinegar is available in white (colourless to pale yellow), black and red varieties from Asian food stores and some supermarkets.

white balsamic

Traditional balsamic vinegar is made with red wine while this variety is made with white wine. It is milder in flavour and is not as sweet as its dark cousin. It is used in sauces and dressings when you don't want a dark balsamic to colour your dish.

white wine

Made from distilled white wine.

wasabi

Wasabi is a very hot Japanese horseradish paste used in making sushi and as a condiment. Available from Asian food stores and supermarkets.

water chestnuts

Edible corms of a water-growing sedge that are popular for their crunchy texture in Chinese cuisine. They're great in stir-fries.

white anchovies

These Spanish anchovies called 'boquerones' are filleted and marinated in white vinegar and olive oil, giving them a sweet, mild taste. They are popular as a tapas dish on their own and are great in robust salads.

white (cannellini) beans

These small, kidney-shaped beans are available from supermarkets either canned or in dried form. Dried beans need to be soaked overnight in water before cooking.

wonton wrappers

Chinese in origin, these square or round thin sheets of dough are available fresh or frozen. They can be steamed or fried. Fill them with meat and vegetables to make dumplings for soup or use as a crunchy base for nibbles, or deep-fry or bake and sprinkle with sugar for dessert.

za'atar

Middle Eastern spice mix containing dried herbs, sesame seeds and sumac. Often used as a crust for grilled and baked meat.

global measures

measures vary from Europe to the US and even from Australia to NZ.

metric & imperial

Measuring cups and spoons may vary slightly from one country to another, but the difference is generally not sufficient to affect a recipe. All cup and spoon measures are level. An Australian measuring cup holds 250ml (8 fl oz).

One Australian metric teaspoon holds 5ml, one Australian tablespoon holds 20ml (4 teaspoons). However, in North America, New Zealand and the UK they use 15ml (3-teaspoon) tablespoons.

When measuring liquid ingredients remember that 1 American pint contains 500ml (16 fl oz), but 1 Imperial pint contains 600ml (20 fl oz).

When measuring dry ingredients, add the ingredient loosely to the cup and level with a knife. Don't tap or shake to compact the ingredient unless the recipe requests 'firmly packed'.

liquids & solids

measuring cups and spoons and a set of scales are great assets in the kitchen.

liquids

cup	metric	imperial
⅛ cup	30ml	1 fl oz
¼ cup	60ml	2 fl oz
⅓ cup	80ml	2½ fl oz
½ cup	125ml	4 fl oz
⅔ cup	160ml	5 fl oz
¾ cup	180ml	6 fl oz
1 cup	250ml	8 fl oz
2 cups	500ml	16 fl oz
2¼ cups	560ml	20 fl oz
4 cups	1 litre	32 fl oz

solids

metric	imperial
20g	½ oz
60g	2 oz
125g	4 oz
180g	6 oz
250g	8 oz
500g	16 oz (1 lb)
1kg	32 oz (2 lb)

made to measure

equivalents for metric and imperial measures and ingredient names.

millimetres to inches

metric	imperial
3mm	⅛ inch
6mm	¼ inch
1cm	½ inch
2.5cm	1 inch
5cm	2 inches
18cm	7 inches
20cm	8 inches
23cm	9 inches
25cm	10 inches
30cm	12 inches

ingredient equivalents

bicarbonate soda	baking soda
capsicum	bell pepper
caster sugar	superfine sugar
celeriac	celery root
chickpeas	garbanzos
coriander	cilantro
cos lettuce	romaine lettuce
cornflour	cornstarch
eggplant	aubergine
green onion	scallion
plain flour	all-purpose flour
rocket	arugula
self-raising flour	self-rising flour
snow pea	mange tout
zucchini	courgette

oven temperature

setting the oven to the right temperature can be critical when making baked goods.

celsius to fahrenheit

celsius	fahrenheit
100°C	200°F
120°C	250°F
140°C	275°F
150°C	300°F
160°C	325°F
180°C	350°F
190°C	375°F
200°C	400°F
220°C	425°F

electric to gas

celsius	gas
110°C	¼
130°C	½
140°C	1
150°C	2
170°C	3
180°C	4
190°C	5
200°C	6
220°C	7
230°C	8
240°C	9
250°C	10

butter & eggs

let 'fresh is best' be your mantra when it comes to selecting dairy goods.

butter

For baking we generally use unsalted butter as it lends a sweeter flavour. Either way, the impact is minimal. Salted butter has a longer shelf life and is preferred by some people. One American stick of butter is 125g (4 oz). One Australian block of butter is 250g (8 oz).

eggs

Unless otherwise indicated we use large (60g) chicken eggs. To preserve freshness, store eggs in the refrigerator in the carton they are sold in. Use only the freshest eggs in recipes such as mayonnaise or dressings that use raw or barely cooked eggs. Be extra cautious if there is a salmonella problem in your community, particularly in food that is to be served to children, the elderly or pregnant women.

the basics

here are some simple weight conversions for cups of common ingredients.

common ingredients

almond meal (ground almonds)
1 cup : 120g
brown sugar
1 cup : 175g
white sugar
1 cup : 220g
caster (superfine) sugar
1 cup : 220g
icing (confectioner's) sugar
1 cup : 160g
plain (all-purpose)
or self-raising
(self-rising) flour
1 cup : 150g
fresh breadcrumbs
1 cup : 70g
finely grated parmesan cheese
1 cup : 80g
uncooked rice
1 cup : 200g
cooked rice
1 cup : 165g
uncooked couscous
1 cup : 200g
cooked, shredded chicken, pork or beef
1 cup : 160g
olives
1 cup : 150g

molten chocolate 182

pumpkin
harissa, and goat's cheese pizza 26
roasted, blue cheese and pear
bruschetta 26

------------------ q ------------------

quesadillas, baked spicy beef 32
quince and apple pork cutlets, roasted 130

------------------ r ------------------

raspberry
and chocolate custards, baked 186
and lemon curd brioche pudding 172
and peach coconut crumble 168
pistachio cakes with rosewater
cream 169
ratatouille tart, free-form 152
red curry roasted vegetables 158
rhubarb and strawberries, roasted, with
whipped mascarpone 166
rice
baked chicken and porcini risotto 60
crispy, and crab omelette 56
ginger fried, with egg 54
lemon, salad with minted lamb 112
noodles with chilli cashews 57
noodle rolls with chilli jam pork 127
pea and mint risotto with crispy
pancetta 54
simple paella 60
thai, with chilli salmon 56
ricotta
asparagus and prosciutto toasts,
roasted 152
egg fritters 15
gnocchi with sage butter, cheat's 40
with pepper and garlic fettucine 46
prosciutto and sage french toast 29
spinach and crispy pancetta bake 158
risotto
baked chicken and porcini 60
pea and mint, with crispy pancetta 54
roasted
apple and quince pork cutlets 130
asparagus, ricotta and prosciutto toasts 152
chicken with pancetta and lentils 82
pumpkin, blue cheese and pear
bruschetta 26

strawberries and rhubarb with whipped
mascarpone 166
tomato, garlic and bread salad 32
vegetable salad with buttermilk
dressing 158

------------------ s ------------------

sage salt steak with pancetta-baked
polenta 96
salad
butter bean, green olive and white
anchovy 68
chicken and fennel, with parmesan
wafers 32
crushed pea, with spiced beef patties 102
grilled chicken, with green chilli ranch
dressing 88
italian veal and herb, with crispy capers 102
lemon rice, with minted lamb 112
olive and rocket, with grilled lamb 110
potato and horseradish, with grilled
lemon snapper 144
prawn and white bean 71
preserved lemon, lentil and
fried tomato 70
preserved lemon and zucchini, with
sesame-crusted salmon 138
roasted tomato, garlic and bread 32
roasted vegetable, with buttermilk
dressing 158
shaved beef and celery, with bloody
mary dressing 98
smashed chickpea with chorizo 70
smoked trout and fennel niçoise 141
swiss chard, with goat's cheese
croutons 152
thai shredded egg 12
three pea, with feta pastries 154
tomato and mint, with balsamic steaks 102
tuna and edamame, with chilli ponzu
dressing 144
tzatziki, with spice-baked chicken 82
warm parsnip, with lamb racks 110
salmon
chilli, with thai rice 56
and dill pie 140
sesame-crusted, with preserved lemon
and zucchini salad 138
salt and pepper
chicken, stir-fried, with coriander
noodles 88

chilli tofu with soy noodles 60
salted caramel and chocolate tarts,
cheat's 180
sandwiches, toasts and bruschetta
goat's cheese croutons with swiss chard
salad 152
lemon, caper and tuna grilled
sandwiches 32
parmesan wafers 32
prosciutto, sage and ricotta french
toast 29
roasted asparagus, ricotta and prosciutto
toasts 152
roasted pumpkin, blue cheese and pear
bruschetta 26
simple chicken schnitzel sandwich 26
smashed pea, goat's cheese and egg
bruschetta 18
sauces, dressings and condiments
bitter chocolate cream 183
bloody mary dressing 98
chilli cashews 57
chilli ponzu dressing 144
chunky rocket pesto 46
coriander and lime dressing 71
creamy tuna dressing 102
green chilli ranch dressing 88
horseradish cream 18
lemon and dill dressing 141
lime and coconut dressing 88
pickled carrot 130
slaw 26
tzatziki salad 82
sausage and lentil cassoulet 74
semifreddo, chocolate 180
sesame-crusted salmon with preserved
lemon and zucchini salad 138
shaved beef and celery salad with bloody
mary dressing 98
simple
chicken schnitzel sandwich 26
paella 60
skewers
maple mustard lamb 116
spiced yoghurt grilled chicken 82
vietnamese pork 130
smashed
chickpea salad with chorizo 70
pea, goat's cheese and egg
bruschetta 18
smoked
ham and potato hash with poached eggs 18
trout and fennel niçoise salad 141

snapper, grilled lemon, with potato and
horseradish salad 144
soft egg and crispy pancetta pasta 12
sorbet, dark chocolate 180
soufflé omelette 14
soup
chicken, chilli and lemon couscous 74
chicken spoon dumpling 85
spiced sweet potato 158
spicy lamb meatball and lentil 74
sourdough chicken pies 28
spaghetti with chunky rocket pesto 46
spice-baked chicken with tzatziki salad 82
spiced
beef patties with crushed pea salad 102
lamb pies 116
sweet potato soup 158
yoghurt grilled chicken skewers 82
spicy
chickpea and chorizo fried eggs 18
lamb meatball and lentil soup 74
one-pot couscous 68
spinach
garlic, with parmesan minute steaks 96
ricotta and crispy pancetta bake 158
steak
balsamic, with tomato and mint salad 102
mustard, with horseradish rösti 98
parmesan minute, with garlic spinach 96
prosciutto-wrapped, with mushroom and
leek tarts 99
sage salt, with pancetta-baked polenta 96
stir-fried salt and pepper chicken with
coriander noodles 88
stir-fry, garlic pepper beef 102
strawberry
lychee and mint granita 168
and rhubarb, roasted, with whipped
mascarpone 166
summer caprese lasagne 43
sweet potato
and pork curry 124
spiced, soup 158
swiss chard salad with goat's cheese
croutons 152

-------------------- t --------------------

tart(s)
cheat's chocolate and salted caramel 180
feta pastries with three pea salad 154
free-form ratatouille 152

mushroom and leek, with prosciutto-
wrapped steaks 99
thai
poached chicken 88
rice with chilli salmon 56
shredded egg salad 12
-style baked fish 144
three pea salad with feta pastries 154
thyme-crumbed veal cutlets 99
toasts − see sandwiches, toasts and
bruschettas
tofu, chilli salt and pepper, with soy
noodles 60
tomato
blt pasta 46
chorizo and basil pasta 40
fried, preserved lemon and lentil salad 70
olive and mozzarella meatballs 96
and mint salad with balsamic steaks 102
roasted, garlic and bread salad 32
trout, smoked, and fennel niçoise salad 141
tuna
and edamame salad with chilli ponzu
dressing 144
lemon and caper grilled sandwiches 32

-------------------- V --------------------

veal
and herb salad, italian, with crispy
capers 102
thyme-crumbed, cutlets 99
vegetable
curry puffs, big 155
red curry roasted 158
roasted, salad with buttermilk dressing 158
vietnamese pork skewers 130

-------------------- W --------------------

white bean and prawn salad 71
wontons, crispy pork 127

-------------------- y --------------------

yoghurt
passionfruit fool 172
spiced, grilled chicken skewers 82

-------------------- Z --------------------

zucchini
mint and haloumi fritters 155
and preserved lemon salad with sesame-
crusted salmon 138

thank you

The words 'thank you' never seem big enough after completing
the enormous task of putting a cook book together. This is for the
photographer, cooks, designers, word wizards, supporters and
my team, who have all helped grease the wheels of progress!

The biggest thank you one could ever imagine goes to my photographer,
William. His attention to detail, sheer precision, beautiful light, all-round
tech geekiness and sense of humour brought the recipes to life and
kept me sane throughout the long days of shooting.

To recipe wrangler, Hannah, thank you for contributing your knowledge,
sheer hard work and organisational skills. You were important in keeping
me on track and forever pushing me forward to meet that deadline!

To the most amazing design duo – Gen and Hayley. What you add to the
book, I am forever grateful for. Thank you for perfectly balancing every
single image and giving the design of this book a perfect flow.

Words in precise instruction and measure, words in whimsy, words on
why you need to buy this book. Mel, you have it all. Thank you for the
mountainous task that is editing and proofreading a cook book.

Dolores and Kirsten, thank you for helping with the recipes and giving
up part of your weekends to keep me on time. And to my magazine staff,
thank you again for your support during book season. I know it's tough.

To my amazing friends and my beautiful little boys, who make
my life complete – thank you, Thank You, THANK YOU!

Thank you to the following suppliers for their wares: Citta, Collect Gallery,
Keiko Matsui, Koskela, Pure and General, Space Furniture, Spence & Lyda.

bio

At the age of eight, Donna Hay skipped into a kitchen, picked
up a mixing bowl and never looked back. She later moved to the
world of magazine test kitchens and publishing, where she
established her trademark style of simple, smart and seasonal
recipes all beautifully put together and photographed.

It is food for every cook, every food-lover, every day and
every occasion. Her unique style turned her into an international
food-publishing phenomenon as a best-selling author of 21 cookbooks,
publisher of the bi-monthly *donna hay magazine*, weekly newspaper
columnist, creator of homewares and a food range, and shop owner
of the donna hay general store in Sydney, Australia.

Books by Donna Hay include *a cook's guide, fast, fresh, simple.,
Seasons, off the shelf, modern classics, the instant
cook, instant entertaining* and *the simple essentials* collection.

donnahay.com

----

donnahay.com

To find more donna hay cook books, recipes
and homewares go to www.donnahay.com
and find us on Facebook and Twitter.